The Whole Kit and Caboodle is...
As Sacred As
1, 2, 3

by
Du' Tsu
Spring Frog

This book is a work of non-fiction. Unless otherwise noted, the author and the publisher make no explicit guarantees as to the accuracy of the information contained in this book and in some cases, names of people and places have been altered to protect their privacy.

The Whole Kit And Caboodle Is… As Sacred As 1,2,3 Copyright © 2006 by Du'Tsu (Elizabeth G. M. Richie). All Rights Reserved.

First published by Author House 05/10/06

Second Edition Self-Published in eBook and Paperback by the Author, Du'Tsu, Elizabeth G. M. Richie, with the assistance of Hyperspace Internet Technologies, Inc., 1308 Stockton Hill Road, Suite A177, Kingman, AZ 86401, hyperspaceit.com, 07/30/2020

Cover design by Hyperspace Internet Technologies, Inc. All rights reserved.

No part of this book may be used or reproduced in any manner whatsoever without written permission except in the case of brief quotations embodied in critical articles and reviews.

For information please address Du'Tsu (Elizabeth G. M. Richie). dustydancer@frontier.com

Library of Congress Control Number: 2020913795
ISBN (e-book): 978-0-578-73119-3
ISBN (paperback): 978-0-578-73118-6

With Appreciation To:

My Celtic, Pagan-Christian ancestors;
The person I met in the library who taught me of paradox: Peter
The four Beloveds who have passed to Spirit:
Larry—my co-adventurer in living 6 years in a root cellar
without electricity and running water—
and sharer of 30 years of precious family life;
Elijah-my way too soon lost sweetheart son;
and my gentle hearted parents, Samuel and Isabel;
And the Beloveds I cherish here on Earth, including
My dear, dear son, Isaiah, and his wonderful family;
The astounding Grandmother Pa'Ris'Ha, who keeps me in the Fire;
And my Beloved, Donovan, who can't seem to finish my book,
and its been six years now

(2020 Preface)
Keep It Simple

Keep God simple. Haha! Nothing like an ambitious undertaking! But here, my friends, is my stab at explaining in a simple manner, the Unexplainable. Never mind that so many folks don't accept the notion of the actual existence of anything like a "God." Really--why bother explaining?

But then, there is LOVE!

Love is so very, very wonderful. So very, very cool. So very, very exciting! So very, very powerful.

OMG! I love LOVE with a passion! Holy Mother of Pearl!

So what if God is Love?

You cannot deny the existence of Love. However you may define it, almost everyone can say that they have had, at the very least, a taste of Love. So that means that you have tasted God! (Or maybe, sadly, you have not tasted love but at least know others who have.)

If God is really and truly Love and Love exists, then God Exists. It's as simple as that. God=Love.

Scientists use mathematical formulas to explain the nature of things. That's why, in this book, I use some simple, basic and very ancient mathematical concepts.

There's been a lot of water under the dam since I completed the original version of **The Whole Kit and Caboodle Is...As Sacred as 1,2,3**. In my opinion, the need for this book is ever more critical today. We earthlings MUST come to terms with our destiny, and God/Love plays a significant role in that destiny. We need to have the conversation about what it means to be human. And the fact is, you are The Chosen and you are Divine!

I have said, You are gods;
all of you are children
of the most High.

from The Bible, Psalm 82:16

Like a Procession you walk
together towards your god-self.

from The Prophet by Kahlil Gibran

You are Chosen,
lest You would not be Here.

Grandmother Pa'Ris'Ha

The Chosen

Celebrate! Humanity is destined for divinity! We are on our way to becoming free, responsible, self-conscious, ever-living, ever-loving citizens in an ethereal Divine cosmos. Believe it or not, we are fated to be magnificent Co-Creators with the Divine Spirit that Creates all things. We are "The Chosen."

Many of "The Chosen" are wandering about in a daze, "with dust in their eyes." Therefore, this One called Du'Tsu (pronounced Too N' Twah) has authored ***The Whole Kit and Caboodle Is...As Sacred As 1,2,3.*** She has come to all People to rebirth the purity and light in mankind. As a herald who sings with wild abandon of a springtime of light and love, her name means "Spring Frog."

If you call yourself a Christian, I challenge you to have the wisdom, courage and respect to withhold sweeping judgements about this book until you've given it a thorough once-over. Likewise, if you are a non-Christian, I would certainly ask and expect no less.

The bottom line message of this book is as follows: When "Christ" in the form of godlike, caring, brotherly, motherly, fatherly, sisterly love finally lives in the hearts, minds and will of men and women across the globe, the prophecy of the "Second Coming" will be fulfilled. Whether that love is inspired by Buddhist piety, Muslim devotion, Hindu wisdom, secular humanism, voodoo economics or Christian passion makes no difference. It will be Love Incarnate that counts. When the Spirit of the one true universal law of love is fulfilled, not the Letter of any particular worldly law or rule, scripture or doctrine, we will have achieved a major goal of human life. This will be called "Good." And we will be well on our way toward achieving divinity.

Christians are taught how very wrong the ancient Hebrews were to expect a warrior savior rather than a gentle, soul/spiritual savior. I would suggest that many modern Christians are now wrongly depending on a "Second Coming" in the bodily person of Jesus. In fact, I think Jesus is alive and well. Nevertheless, it is "Christ in You" that must be the real "Second Coming." And this kind of "Second Coming" is simply another way to say that humanity is destined for divinity.

Humans often associate the term, "divinity," with both supernatural powers and forms as well as exceptional moral greatness. Thus it shall be in this book. I assert that the human race is destined for moral purity, exemplary wisdom, and awesome capabilities. Further, I propose that the human being and the earth are evolving together toward an "ethereal" form, one which is more akin to light and energy than to the substance we now call "material."

Such notions are common fare in spiritual discussions but legitimate science regularly belittles them. So this book also addresses the rift between science and religion...for indeed, it is this rift in humanity's explanations of itself that must be bridged in order for the evolution of humanity's divinity to come to fruition.

Now, allow me to tell you a little about myself.

I had a powerful mystical experience when I was 18 years old. For roughly a week's time, I experienced love as if it were bombarding me from all directions, as if every physical thing was made of a radioactive element emitting love.

Every cloud, every leaf on every tree, and every stone on the ground or lodged in an ivy covered wall--that is to say-- every substance was a sun unto itself, emanating love.

Indeed, at that ripe old age of 18, I came to see that humans were—for the most part—totally oblivious to the profundity and reality of the "ground of the universe"—the Love that underpins everything.

At the time, I said that I was "Born again in Christ." But the experience went beyond a specific religion because the Christ, the Spirit of Love, transcends any one religious doctrine. No one people or tradition holds the exclusive rights to love. How could they?

I am also quite confident that both Science and Religion will one day totally embrace these ideas.

But today as in 1972, humanity does not act in accordance or "at One" with the logic of love, the Logos. Humans have the choice to act Divinely and give love or to act profanely and not to give love. Or rephrased, we all have the choice to prolong the agony of separation from Love, or to live in the passion of being One with it.

In 1975 I earned a BA in the academic study of religion. I have followed a winding but always enriching path ever since. I've hung back silently for a long time. But now, this One called Du'Tsu shall "tell it like it is."

Sooner or later, we the Created MUST come full circle and acknowledge the Divine Loving Creator in ourselves and in all other things. It's an ancient Truth that—apparently—must be spoken a hundred zillion times or more because humans are so thick headed. It's a Truth that defies the barriers between Catholic and Protestant, Muslim and Jew and so on; and is as factual as any scientific "fact."

If you accept what I write in *The Whole Kit and Caboodle Is...As Sacred As 1,2,3,* you will understand that Truth is both simple and complex and such a mysterious paradox! We are a species, born out of the Divine. We are evolving toward a divine future by pulling ourselves up by our own flimsy bootstraps denying our destiny all the while.

So, I now present this sweeping theological frolic to the family of humanity, the children of the Most High, to every human being. These shocking Revelations are for pompous windbags and self-righteous critics; for half a brain rednecks and no-brainer snobs; for blue bloods and HIV positives; for rosy cheeked crones and lovable old codgers; for clueless, alienated, teens, cynical scientists and wizened, wheezing academics; for obsessive golfers and bikers; for bridge players, antique car collectors, college students and dropouts; for wall flowers, perverts, deviants and hateful killers; for hillbillies, hairdressers, and cosmopolites; for rich men, poor women, beggars, thieves, doctors, lawyers and indecent cheats; for Blacks, Reds, Whites, Blues, Yellows and Greens; for Arabs and artists, and arch fundamentalists; for arch liberals, arch enemies, arch conservatives, and arch dukes; arch fiends, architects, archaeologists, archbishops, archers and archetypal New Agers; for nostalgic hippies, the baby boomers and Generation Whatevers; for materialistic slobs, hot raunchy rappers and nice or obnoxious talk show hosts; for xenophobes, Zorastrians and zymologists (those who study fermentaion.) It is <u>especially</u> for Americans who <u>claim</u> to be of the Christian creed.

I try not to use too many big words because I want to give EVERYONE a chance to understand. I am purposely repetitive because humanity is a STUBBORN, stiff-necked, bone-headed lot. I SHOULD KNOW. I'M ONE OF US!

And now, without further adieu, allow me to introduce you to yourself..............

Heeere's God..........!!!!

The One

"So God created man in his own image, in the image of God he created him; male and female he created them."
The Bible   Genesis: 1:27

What if God was One of Us?
Just a slob like one of us?
Just a stranger on a bus
Trying to make His way home?
Words by Eric Bazilian
and performed by Joan Osbourn

Why doesn't someone just come out and say it!
God IS One of Us.
God IS Every One of Us.
...There I said it.
Elizabeth Richie

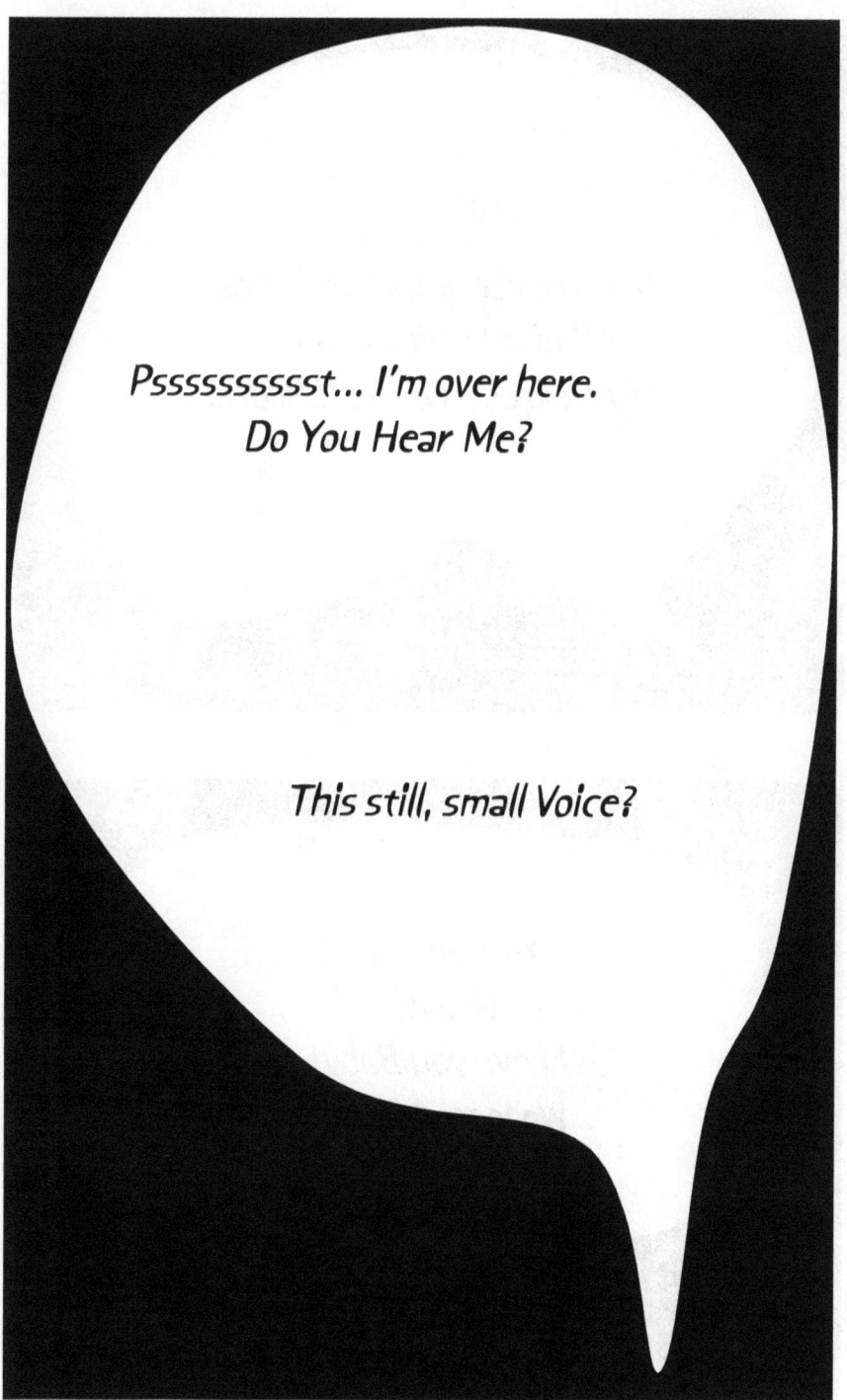

Allow Me to introduce
Myself, personally....
My Name is

Well, that's just one of my names.
**I have thousands of names, millions,
trillions, godzillions!**
But for now, just call me
Spirit Divine. Okay?
Read my lips.

Many people are lousy at remembering names so I
want to braze **MINE** into your brain.

I AM Spirit Divine

I AM NOT
going to beat around the bush.

I AM also

The One and Only GOD.

I AM Spirit Divine And GOD.

Got That?
Now, close your eyes.

Now open them again.
What did you see? Did You see **ME**?
Try again...Did you see Spirit Divine?

Most folks don't see me
in the Darkness.
For that matter, most folks don't see Me
in the Light, either.
Do You?

Where can I be seen?

The Fact is......

OnlyTrue Seekers
can find Me.

But you have been told in sacred text:
"The Kingdom of God is within You."
(Luke 17:21)

So close your eyes tightly this time and take a closer look.

What did you find in there?
Pretty pictures, crazy ideas,
guilty or lustful thoughts?
Voices that say cynically,
"God in Me? Yeah, Right!"
Reverence, awe, brilliancy?
Darkness, babble, confusion, stupidity?

Did You Find God Within Yourself?

Yes? No? Maybe?
Take a deep breath and listen carefully.
I AM going to make a statement that goes against all tradition and authority.

Prepare Ye the Way For Divine Revelation!

*To find Me,
Spirit Divine,
you need look no farther
than The Darkness!*
I hope this doesn't scare you too much,
but the Truth is,

I AM the DARKNESS.

EEEEEEK!!!
Horror of Horrors!
No, No!
A Thousand
Times No!
What
Blasphemy!

Forgive Me, but it's True.

I Am the Darkness.

I AM...the inky blackness of the place behind your eyes. I Am the velvety dark robe of midnight...I am ultraviolet energies and the sable expanses of space. I Am the awesome mystery and power of a Black Hole. I Am the Dark Matter and Dark Energy of which your advanced Scientists speak.

I AM the sweet, dark, rich loam of the earth and the iridescent raven's wing.

I Am the Great Void.

I AM

the King and Queen of Darkness!

Please allow me to explain, beginning with a new vocabulary word.

EEEEEEK!!! Horror of Horrors! No, No! A Thousand Times No! Not a New Word!

Worse things could certainly happen.
I could give you a toothache you know.
Ahem...
The New Word is "Ineffable."
(Pronounced like "Effie" as in "good ole Aunt Effie" and "Bull" as in "Bless her heart. We don't mind talking with Aunt Effie even if we aren't interested **in-Effie-Bull.**"
......Ha ha ha....................No seriously.....
Doest thou wish to consult a
lower authority? i.e. Webster?

<u>**Ineffable**—**1. Too overwhelming to be expressed in words: incapable of being expressed in words: indescribable 2. Too sacred to be spoken 3. Unspeakable,**</u>
taboo.

I AM the Ineffable DARKNESS.

You see, for centuries, people have oft said that God is too vast, too mysterious and too awesome to understand. This is what "ineffable" means.
Many have said that God is indescribable. Thus it is that Native Americans have a word for ME that means "The Great Mystery." Strange name, eh?
Yes indeed. I have had many, many names because many think that
NO ONE WORD
can fully describe Me.
I have had special names that no one was allowed to say except perhaps the high priests...on special occasions. This helped to maintain an aura of respect and power about the most Holy thing in the universe,

God....Spirit Divine.

Alas, far too often My Name or Names have been exploited and used for ignoble, shameful, corrupt purposes. I fume when I think about it.
It's been criminal. It's been loathsome and tragic.
Humanity is Now Sadder but Wiser.

NOW, I WANT YOU TO TALK ABOUT ME! GO AHEAD. BLAB! TALK UP A STORM!

Pssssst. Did you hear what I heard about Spirit Divine? You just won't believe it!

Anything is better than being ignored!
Your Ignore---ance is soooo yucky!

Humanity is ready to understand the Ineffable!

NOW—if you do talk about **ME**,
--I know most of you will **not** say
that God --Spirit Divine--is the Darkness.
You don't like to pair
God and Darkness. Right?
I mean, like, you can't help but think of EVIL
and witches in black hats, or Satan when you put
"darkness" and anything "spiritual"
together in the same thought. The Christian
tradition, which dominates spiritual thinking in
America, calls the Devil
"The Prince of Darkness." Right?
But, who is the <u>king</u>?
ME of Course...Spirit Divine!
Like I said...
I Am the King and Queen of Darkness!

Alas....The Darkness Has Such a Lousy Reputation

*Moreover,
most of you are really and truly afraid of the dark!
(Your film industry has guaranteed that.) So you have a
hard time treating darkness with calm reason.
And I certainly don't want you to just blindly and
stupidly accept as Gospel that
I AM the Darkness.
Of course,*

You probably don't believe that God is truly talking to you in this
book, let alone that I Am the Darkness,
but please bear with Me!
I will be patient and I won't even threaten you
with a thunderbolt just yet. No, I've tried scaring people into
believing stuff and it just ain't cool.

No, No, No.
I want that light-bulb
in your head to go on.

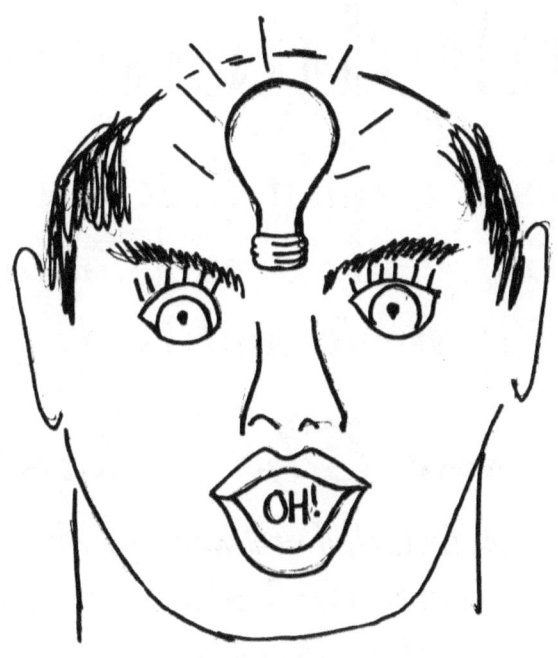

I WANT YOU TO
SEE THE LIGHT!

I want you to See the profound
Light of Logic. I want you to
Understand without a shadow of a
doubt. I want you to
Feel the Power of the Truth!

I Want You to Become...

Enlightened!

Indeed, Ultimately, it is your
Destiny As My Grand Children
To Really and Truly

Become The Light!

In a very real, factual, literal way, you will become
Ethereal beings, as refined as the sunlight.
But First Things First...
First the Mind, then the Matter,
Mental/Spiritual Enlightenment will be the Focus

here...so....Look into your Mind....

Glory Alleluia, Children of Darkness!
Close those peepers again!

What's inside that thick skull of yours?
When you close your eyes,
it gets Dark, right?
No artificial lighting in there, right?
Don't deny it!.....But take comfort.

That Darkness is ME!

Today, it may also be a Darkness filled with stupidity, of not knowing, of ignorance. It may be a darkness that is full of confusion and chaos, or slow, lazy thoughts, or paranoia, hatred, depression, or worry, anger or anxiety. Hopefully, you are not as bad off emotionally as all that.

But whoever you are, whether you are a genius or an average Joe, a happy camper or a depressed alcoholic, it's dark in there. If you walk upon this earth as a human being, inside that head of yours is a darkness and a mystery,...

A <u>Great</u> Dark Mystery.
And that <u>Mystery</u> is Me.
Yet Far Too Many of You
Deny My Presence,
and Feel Like Lost Souls..........

In any case, by the time *I AM* finished here, I want that spongy, cauliflower substance behind your eye sockets to catch a glimpse of the blissful light of true knowledge. Ideally, I want you to be orgasmically aroused—downright titillated ---with the awesome passion of understanding.

If, by the time *I AM* finished here,
You can say with your eyes closed that

"The Darkness Comprehends the Light"—

One of My Wildest Dreams and Most
Ambitious Goals for
You will Be Accomplished!

In more ways than One
Am I The Darkness...
So for now, set the notion that

"I AM the Darkness"

on the back burner of your brain,
primitively illustrated thusly:

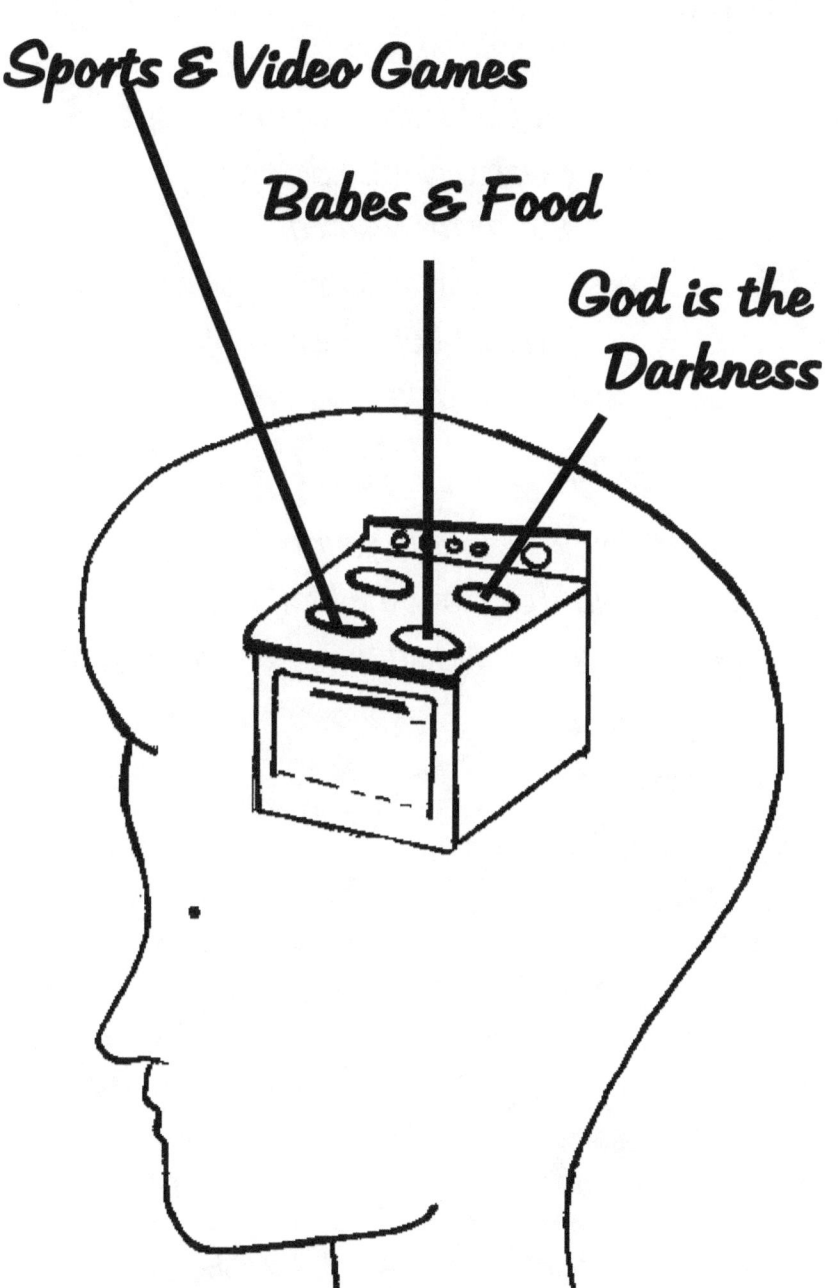

NOW, with yet another sweeping and astounding
PROCLAMATION,
Let Us Boldly Go Where Spiritual Wimps
Have Dared Not Go Before!
But be forewarned.
This won't be the last strange and dubious notion
I will set before you,
so I am urging you now.

Don't say "no," just say "oh."

Ponder things in your heart,
just as it is said that Mary the Mother of Jesus did
the night the shepherds told her of angels on high...

You can say "NO" at the end of the book if you want.
But if you are patient, all will become clear.
Don't close the window to the Light just yet.
OK?????——OK.
So I say it again.
I AM the Darkness.
And of course,
though you may not believe this either,

I AM The Light.

In fact, the Profound, Paradoxical
Truth of the Matter Is,
The Awesome and Vital
Information that the Human World
<u>Must Ultimately Embrace is that</u>

I Am Everything!

Read the Holy Lips again:

Don't say "No," just say "Oh!"
Give your brain some mulling time.
Don't pull closed the window blinds.

I Am The Darkness
and
I Am The Light!!!

I AM Spirit Divine.
I AM God.

AND...........INDEED.......

I AM absolutely, positively
every itsy bitsy, teeny weeny,
yellow polka dot bikini
as well as
All the Known and Unknown
Universes, Galaxies, Astral
Planes and Dimensions.

I AM
the birds, the bees,
the flowers, the trees,
the moon up above and

I Am

LOVE.

EEEEEEEKKKK!!!!!!!!
What in Heaven's
Name
does Spirit Divine
mean by saying
"I AM EVERY
GOSH DARN
THING"?

Well, what else could I BE?
Consider the two little words,

"I AM,"

and check out the Bible. Exodus 3:13-14—

Then Moses said to God, "If I go to the Israelites and tell them that the God of their forefathers has sent me to them, and they ask me his name, what shall I say?

God answered, "I AM; that is who I Am. Tell them that [the] 'I AM' has sent you to them."

Yes!!! (Yea, Verily)
First and foremost, fundamentally and essentially,

I AM THE "I AM."

Again you wonder:
What is the Almighty Spirit talking about?

Look at it this way. Another way to say
"I AM" is to say: "I Exist."
If everything that exists could sing out
the Truth or Fact of its existence,
each thing would say

"I AM."

Consider yourself.... If you wished to say to someone
that you existed,
you could say:

"<u>I AM.</u>"

Simply stated...

"I AM" means
"I Exist."

Neil Diamond was echoing **ME** in his song:
"I AM, I cried....I AM, says I.
But no one heard not even the chair..."

In the First and Last Analysis,
The Truth of the Matter is,
Believe It Or Not:
**I AM THE <u>ONLY</u> THING
THAT <u>DOES</u> EXIST.**
You and every other thing in the whole wide universe, living or dead, visible and invisible, are just parts of
ME...Spirit Divine...GOD.
You and everything else are simply fingers, arms, legs, heart, hands, feet, nose and boogies of the body of
Spirit Divine.

SOOOOOO.....
WAKE UP AND DIE RIGHT!

I AM
the
I AM.

And I AM going to drive this point
right into your multi-dimensional,
dimwitted noggins until
you're sick of it.........
Ad nauseum. (Until you vomit.)
Ad infinitum...(Forever and Ever,)
Even unto the End of this Book.

You ask........ **Why?**

BECAUSE THIS IS THE
MOST IMPORTANT
IDEA IN RECENT
UNIVERSAL HISTORY.

✸✸✸✸✸✸

*In This Apocalyptic Moment in
Human Evolution...*
*THIS IS THE KEY to YOUR
VERY OWN EXISTENCE!
YOU AND I, Spirit Divine, ARE
INEXORABLY LINKED!*

✱✱✱

*THIS IS THE SOLUTION
TO THE HUMAN DILEMMA:*

All that Is in the Universe is

Spirit
Divine!

Fundamentally, in the final analysis of everything that exists including EVERY HUMAN BEING....
There is Nothing Else
But Spirit Divine.
???????
IF YOU Think There Is,
Think Again....

I Will Let You In on Little Secret!

Once upon a time...Way back "In the Beginning," when I was about to begin creating the known and unknown universes, I looked around and saw that there weren't any substances or materials to use to create the Creation. That is, there was nothing but a Void, so to speak, a Great Mystery. There was **Nothing but ME**, (GOD-the Spirit Divine) in the whole wide universe. It was Quite a Puzzle; Just Me--

--Ineffable Darkness--
Everywhere.
Who can say what
I ACTUALLY WAS?
So......What was I to do?
No lumber or hardware stores anywhere! No quarks. No black holes. No bubbles of energy. No whatever else your scientists think came first. There was Nothing but Me......

So, what could I USE to

Do My Thing

and Create the Universe?

I Was the One and Only Thing that Was!

?????What to do?????

?????What to do?????

SO...By Jove!
I AM SO CLEVER!

I USED <u>MY OWN BODY</u>
TO CREATE THE UNIVERSE!

*I used My Own Body
to Create
the Creation.
"Bang!" says I.
Or, in other words,
"Let There Be Light!"*

Let there be cosmic bubbling and superstrings and holographic patterns and waves, 144,000 dimensions, webs and resonating, harmonic frequencies of energy and atoms, swirling nebulae and baby black holes, universes and galaxies, etc. etc. etc.

*WHATEVER.......
And that's just the
Beginning of the Story.*

The POINT IS---What came forth,
Came forth <u>OUT of Me</u>—
<u>The Great Mystery, The Source.</u>
Therefore:
The universe is the
Flesh of MY FLESH.
Its substance is
MY SUBSTANCE.
Its being is MY BEING.
Its existence is
MY EXISTENCE.
Its power is My Power.

etc. etc. etc.

ALL THAT IS, IS ME.

I am All that Exists.

I AM the

UNIVERSAL EXISTOR.

I Am the One and Only "Ground of the Universe." I Am the Eternal Substance.
I AM All THAT IS—
Material and Immaterial

| I AM | I AM | I AM |
| SPIRIT | ENERGY | MATTER |

I AM CONSCIOUSNESS....I AM DIVINE

THE UNIVERSE IS MY BEING.
MY BEING IS THE UNIVERSE.

All things, substance, material, dimensions, energies, forms, shapes, phenomena, events, and kitchen sinks are an EMANATION of ME,

and therefore, they are ME.
What's an Emanation?
An "Emanation" is something
that comes forth from a source.
I AM THE SOURCE OF ALL THAT IS.
MOST EMPHATICALLY,
ALL THINGS THAT EXIST
ARE COMPOSED OF ME.

I Am the Giver of the Subtance of Being.

INDEED—

I Am
The Universal
Existor.

Yey Verily, I AM THE ESSENCE AND SUBSTANCE OF ALL BEING. I Am What You Are!

Yet you know it not......

ALL THINGS THAT EXIST DO SO BECAUSE
**I MAKE A GIFT
OF MY HOLY BEING**
FOR ALL OTHER BEINGS
AND THINGS IN THE UNIVERSE TO EXIST.
THAT IS WHY I BEGAN
THIS BOOK BY SAYING:
"I have thousands of names,
millions, trillions, godzillions."
Strictly and technically speaking,
**ALL THAT HAS BEEN NAMED
OR WILL BE NAMED—IS ME,**
the Sacred Ground of the Universe,
GOD, SPIRIT DIVINE,
THE ONE AND ONLY

"I AM."

Everything in the Universe Is the Flesh of My Flesh.

All the Universe is ME!

**BELIEVE IT OR NOT,
AT YOUR OWN PERIL.**

YEA, SO BE IT. AMEN

NOW—If you knew God was the
Ground of the Universe,
if you saw this as TRUTH, you would hold the cosmos, the world,
your neighbor, your self and your enemy and every moment in time
in complete reverential
HONOR, AWE and RESPECT.
You would See
All Things As Sacred.
In fact, if you would but REALIZE the truth of this
Truth in the deepest marrow of your
Darkness, and allow it to wash away all
doubt and argument, you would
EXPERIENCE WHAT IS REAL
perhaps for the first time in your life!
You would discover that <u>even</u> the
darkness is made in the Image of God!

The fact is, when any human being
says of themselves,
"I AM," it is as if *I,*
Spirit Divine, **Am** speaking.

No. No.
A thousand times No!
God can't be speaking
through Every
Human Being!
What about
Bad Guys?
What about Evil?
What about little <u>me</u>?
I am definitely
not Holy or Divine!
Give me a break!
Holy Cow!

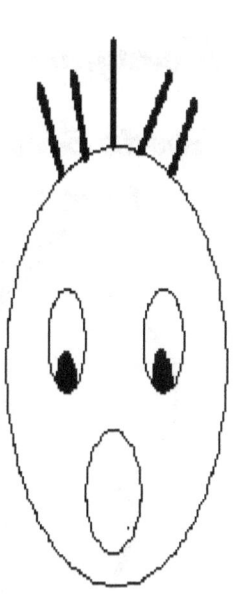

All Human Beings, All Rocks, Plants, Animals--
Every Thing is a part of my Body.

In a while, I will discuss

EVIL.

Put it on the backburner for now.

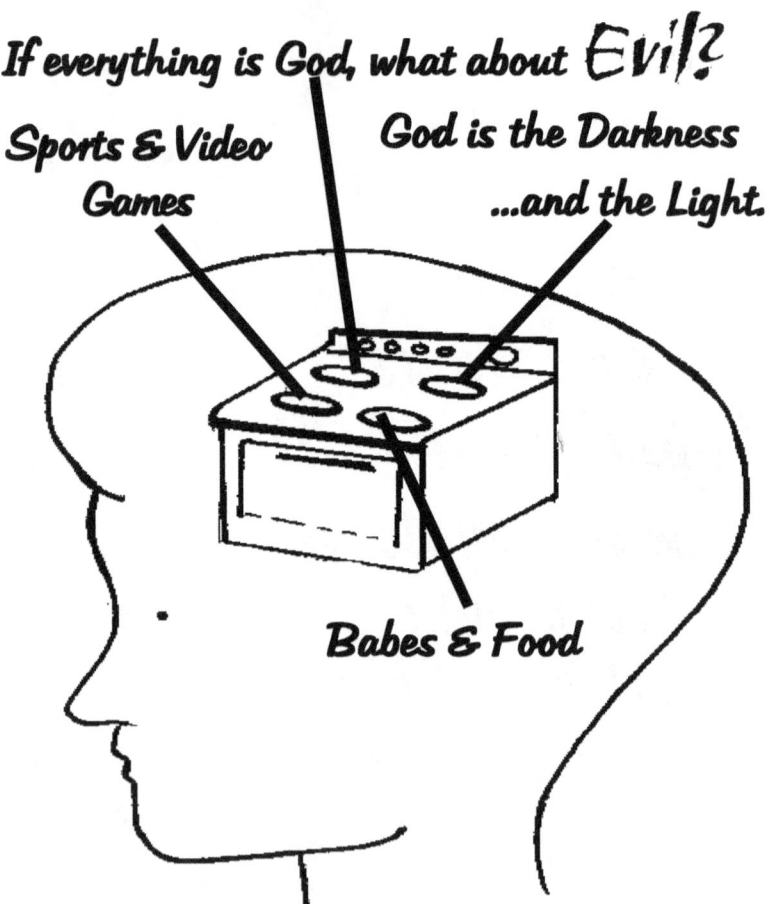

If everything is God, what about Evil?

Sports & Video Games

God is the Darkness ...and the Light.

Babes & Food

For Now, let Us Focus Your Thoughts on the Greatest Good that God Is...

Love.

At my Core...that Is What I Am.

It is humanly possible to harmonize with
ME as the ONE GROUND OF THE WORLD--
to resonate and reverberate to My Core vibrations,
the Essence of My Being, in such a way that
any person can sense a power --ME-- as
a field of energy which can best

be described as
𝕷𝔒𝔙𝔈...

Have you ever Loved...anything or anybody?

If So, then You Have Known God.

A "True Seeker" hungers and thirsts
for NOT just a little taste of love,
a little drop of God,
every now and then.
A "True Seeker" yearns to swim
in the Sea of God--
to be awash in the blissful
Golden Ocean of Love.
Words can hardly describe this
ecstatic state. But some call it--

"Oneness" with God,
others call it

"Enlightenment."

Danger! Will Robbinson!

*Comics, cynics and skeptics,
poke fun at the notion of*
"Oneness with God."
Okay, humor is cool...to a point.
But that Does Not Mean
that such an Experience
is not worthy of your
Deep and Respectful Consideration
BECAUSE
Down Through The Ages,
Prophets, Sages and Saints
Have sought this Dream, (or some form of it)
and have awakened in the Seeking to
"Oneness With God."

In fact,
You--Yourself
COULD Become ONE with ME and BE LOVING AND ILLUMINATED AND AWARE OF THE AWESOME TOTALITY THAT IS ME.
This is the Great Hope of Human Kind.
This is the Call --
the Demand--
of Your Apocalyptic Era.

So Let's Take the Long Way Around and Look at the meaning of "ONENESS."

You will need to learn a little of YE NEW OLDE MATH, *STARTING WITH ZERO..."O"...*

THE PREGNANT CIRCLE

First of all...Allow me to proclaim that modern civilization has lost touch with the meaning, and value of Symbols, except when it comes to commercial logos. Symbols can efficiently convey truths regarding the nature and character of the Universe where words fall short. Further, absolutely essential to humanity is the understanding of

the most basic of symbols,

The Circle.

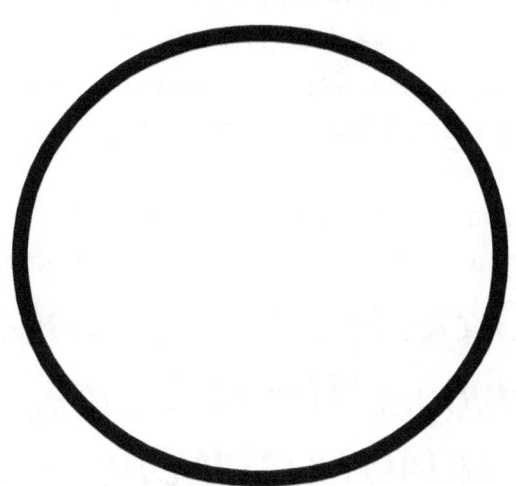

The Circle **symbolically** *represents the Whole, Entire Universe. Why? . . . Because, among other things, the circumference of the circle represents a boundary that if large enough, could encircle the Whole Kit and Caboodle, the entire Universe--*

The Whole Kit and Caboodle

Above is an imaginative picture of the universe, the whole kit and caboodle, including all dimensions, all parallel universes, all kitchen sinks and T.V.s, all heavens, all planets, all hells, all black holes, all itsy bitsy teeny weeny yellow polka dot bikinis, all one eyed, one horned, flying purple people eaters
and all giant dwarf space hamsters.
But we don't really need the cute little pictures.

The Circle, by itself, symbolizes Everything..."The All That Is," and THE QUALITY OF INDIVISIBLE WHOLENESS.

Also, since I--Spirit Divine--Am the entire universe, the Circle represents God.

The Circle Represents the Whole

The Circle symbolizes GOD!

The All That Is

The Circle Illustrates

The Whole
Kit and Caboodle

As a thought exercise...Consider the little Circle that is the Cell in Living Tissue.

In the human body, tissue is made up of little tiny DISTINCT UNITS called cells. Each contains all the fundamental characteristics and processes which are necessary for any particular type of tissue to function. The cells are generally shaped like little circles though their shape may be oblong or squarish. The point is that...inasmuch as a cell contains all the elements that make it perfectly operational— each cell is a complete containment vessel--

a "whole" in miniature.

Thus, Spirit Divine in Nature uses the Circular form to repeatedly and endlessly create Wholly Functional Units!

The Ultimate Wholly, HOLY Functioning Unit is, of course, the Universe

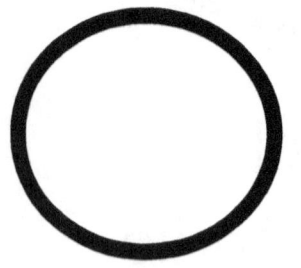

or... "The All That is."

NOW...Notice the uncanny similarities between a Circle and a Zero.
A Zero is simply a long Circle!

A Zero looks like a living cell that is growing and preparing to split and propagate. In a manner of speaking,

a Zero is a pregnant Circle!

Notice how like an Egg (ancient symbol of fertility) it is!
Think of Your Universe! What a wondrous Creation it is! And yet--
what wonders are left still to be created! Think of how much potential there is in the Universe. Think of the vastness and the possibilities!
The Universe Is Full of Potential, Pregnant with possibility!
And if you are one of those naive people (just joking) who believe in so-called Miracles...then Your Universe is even more

Full of Potential!

Poor olde misunderstood, misrepresented Zero!
It doesn't mean "Nothing!"
It represents Everything--the Divine <u>All that Is</u>--
just like the Circle!
But additionally it can illustrate
that the Nature of the Universe is one of
continuing, on-going Creative Potential.

**Mirror Mirror
on the Wall--
Who's the Most
Creative One of All!?**
Don't Count Me (God) Out!

The Cracked Egg History of Numbers

Once upon a time, a few centuries after the demise of Atlantis, the People who went East wanted to measure and count things. The wise ones took to making little squiggles--now called "numbers"--to show

Quantities.

However, the higher they tried to count, the harder it became. Oddly and paradoxically, in order to count higher, they had to figure out how to use the

ZERO!

*Oddly and paradoxically, the invention and use of the
Zero enabled the ancient mathematicians of India to
count higher and to do
Higher Mathematics!
Is that not stranger than strange???!!!
Ha Ha Ha! Adding a Zero to numbers
makes them bigger!*

1 with a zero to its right is 10!

**What the Devil!??!
Oddly and paradoxically,
a squiggle that more accurately
portrays "everything"--
the entire universe--**

came to symbolize "nothing."

**The true meaning of zero
was lost in the mists of Time.**

Zero became what's called a "place holder"--filler, fluff.

*By a strange albeit necessary twist of fate,
in using the zero to represent "nothing,"
ancient mathematicians "reduced" the Zero to a
shadowy reflection of its true symbolic glory.
No longer was it to be the egg, the pregnant Circle, the
symbol of the Whole that is All Things
including Universal Potential.
Rather, it grew to become a squiggle that meant
the Null, the Void, the Nothing.*

Although indeed,
in a manner of speaking
(paradoxically)--truly--
Everything <u>IS</u> Nothing---
because Everything is
<u>No One thing In Particular</u>...
No <u>One</u> Thing But <u>All</u>
Things--God!

Stop it God,
You're just
having too much
fun trying to
confuse me!

Yes, slowly but surely, numbers lost their full symbolic meaning and their spiritual potency.

Today, the meanings of <u>all</u> numbers are associated with the measurement and size of quantities—portions, amounts, values, volume. Mathematics, the language of Science, is commonly used for comparisons, counting, calculations, evaluations and judgments.
Thus Science --because it depends on Mathematics-- has been divorced and alienated from the Ultimate meaning of Things.
This is a degenerate state of affairs.

In the Ancient of Days, Measuring and Quantifying began to take Dominion in this World.
Quantity became Your Sacred Idol, Your GOD!

Quantifying became your obsessive pastime.

Quality became the ever-elusive, unreachable Dream.

But the story is far from over.
Recall (see page 53) that we are working our way toward understanding **"Oneness."**
SOOOO...What squiggle is used to express "One?"

/....1...1...I

the upright line.....

Can you see it now? A chieftan returning from a raid on an enemy tribe, greets his People. Silently he communicates that one in their party has died by raising one finger.

Another ancient wise man wishes to symbolically represent in the sand on the beach how many fish he caught that day. It wasn't such a great day. He caught only "1." Nevertheless, it was a fully functioning, whole, healthy fish. (He had let the big one get away, or he would have had two. But let's not go there yet.) Whether it be a fish or a man, the idea of "one" is easily understood as a singular, whole unit of something.
Cut the tail from the fish, and you no longer have a true fish. Cut the head from a man and no longer do you have a human "unit," a real <u>One</u>.

Separate the Earth from the Sky, the Milky Way from Andromeda, time from space, and you no longer have the <u>Whole</u> Singular Universe--

--The Whole Kit and Caboodle.

Realize that the number "1" does not simply represent the
Quantity of One.
It also represents
the <u>Quality</u> of One...which is

Unity.

A Unity is a Whole Thing, perhaps made of parts-- but it holds together at the seams and if torn asunder, is no longer the same thing.

At first glance you might say,
"The Universe is Not a Unity!"
The universe has so much diversity,
so many things to Name!
BUT TAKE A GOOD LOOK AROUND!
Where are the sharp dividing lines of Separation?
Obviously...in the immortal words
attributed to Chief Joseph...
<u>"All Things are Connected."</u>
Where does outerspace end
and the blue sky begin?
Where does the blue sky end
and the cloud begin?
Where does the sunshine end
and the leaf that turns the sun's energy
into your food begin?
The Universe transforms endlessly like a
restless beast, taking form out of invisible
energies, losing form to another form,
disappearing again into the Unseen and
re-appearing as a cloud, rain,
an ocean, a fish and a tasty meal.
Nothing is destroyed...only Transformed...
Transubstantiated...metamorphosed from
one thing to another.

Therefore...and always...All things
depend on other things
To Exist.
All is a tightly interwoven Unity!
The rocks become the soil that become
the roots that become the stem that
becomes the flower...soaking up
water, air, light.
Nothing lives in separation.
Each apparently separate "thing" in the
universe is intimately linked or connected
to something else which is intermeshed
with something else which is
derived from something else,
which is born from something else,
ad infinitum, for eternity.
And all is ultimately derived from the
same SOURCE.
Look at this Inter-connected, Inter-linked,
Interfused, Integrated, Inter-dependent
massive universe, and understand this:
There is One and only One, single,
Unified, crazily connected Whole Unit
that is the Universe.
THIS I AM!

The Universe is The One and Only Divine Unity, the Unity That is God.

So you see, symbolically speaking...

The Truth Is:
0 = 1

Zero equals One!
The Divine Whole that is Everything--
the Universe as symbolized by a elongated
Circle or Zero -- "0"--
is Identical To or Equal -- "="--
to a Singular, Indivisible,
Tightly Woven Unified Unit,

symbolized by the number "1."
And...Fact is Stranger than fiction! 0=1

Can You Believe?

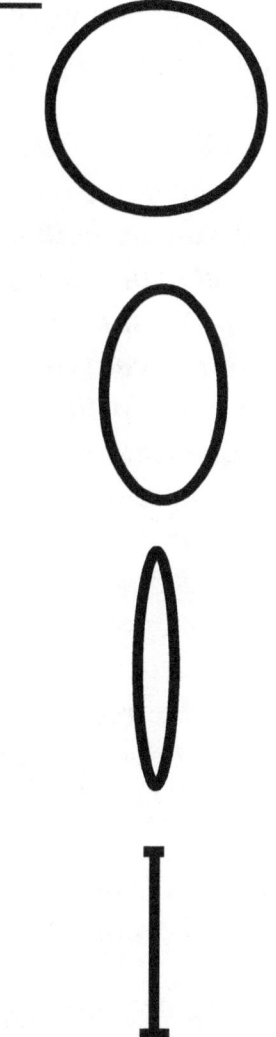

Can you Believe that
In the universe, although
I AM All that Exists,
I take many forms...
Thus, *I AM* All This--
Atoms and energy, most emphatically,
 both are the same;
Birds and bees, the same substance They;
The kitchen sink, flowers and trees,
Elephants and ruthless thieves;
Skyscrapers, worn out shoes;
Infidels and kangaroos;
Mountains, oceans, deserts, sky,
Mother Earth and apple pie.
SPIRIT DIVINE, *I AM*
THE ONE, THE ALL,
THE WHOLE, THE MANY,
A million bucks, a single penny.
What you see and don't see
is what *I IS*.
To awaken to this is Bliss.
....Thus spake Spirit Divine.

I hope you have understood the consequences of what **I** have been explaining to you. That is... <u>If everything in the Universe is Spirit Divine, this includes every human being.</u>
<u>Hence, YOU ARE DIVINE BABY! YOU. YOU. YOU!</u>

Frequently Asked Questions

Q: If everything in the universe is Divine and I am Divine and a Tree is Divine, what makes me different from a tree?

A: Obviously there are many, many differences between you and a tree and We'd need a book to speak of them all. But you are both the same inasmuch as you are part and parcel of the Sacred, Holy, Divine Whole.

The most profound difference, perhaps, is found in the **realm of consciousness**. *The consciousness of a tree does not exist in the material world in the same way your consciousness does. Here on earth, you can say "I AM" while a tree can not. Or so it seems.*

However, there is a realm that exists where a tree has a voice and can say "I Am." Or said another way, there is a state of grace in which you can exist and actually hear the tree speak. In any case, as a part of the Divine Body of God, the tree is sacred and definitely should be treated with all due respect. And some-day...who knows......maybe you will hear it speak.

Q: What's the big deal with this "I Am" stuff? And how could I ever be "One With God?"

A: The "I AM" is the quality of God that declares its self-existence. If you can say "I Am," you are announcing your own existence. (We will talk about this alot in the Chapter on The Three.)

Few appreciate the remarkable gift that is the ability to say "I Am." This ability requires the power of consciousness to reflect upon the self, to SEE one's own self. Then a being must have both the will and power to reflect back into the universe with a Voice.

Humans are blessed with the capacity to reflect upon the self. Too few, however, consider the question that comes with deep self-reflection: "What the heck Am I?" The final answer can be nothing other than the realization that "I Am a reflection and incarnation of the Divine One."

Right now, you may believe you are limited to being a thinking brain within a physical body that dies with the death of the body. You may also believe your powers of thought are limited by genetics, or by education or some such thing. But the fact is, the "I AM" in you does not have to abide by any of these limitations. The fact is, you could access every part of the universe--your full, rightful body-- any time you might desire. As a very wise Grandmother has often said,

"You are not in the Universe, the Universe is in You."

When you awaken to this experience, you will know what it feels to be "One with God."

Imagine realizing that <u>your</u> Spirit actually reaches to the far ends of the Universe and into the great depths of hidden Wisdoms and complex dimensions, past, present and future. Such would be Oneness with what is called God, "The All that Is."

Indeed, the human being has quite a unique status in the universe inasmuch as a human is an ALTAR for the fullest, and potentially the most highly evolved expression of the Divine One.

"Expanding" and aligning the Circle (or sphere) that is You with the Circle (or sphere) that is the whole Universe, awakening to the fact that you are Identical.....this is the goal. Then the Divine will live through you most fully.

Of course there is a big difference between thinking you understand the concept of Oneness and actually **experiencing** the bliss of being "One with God." You can agree philosophically with the possibility of "Oneness with God" before it happens to you. In fact, this is an essential first step.

My recommendation is this. You can strive to go with the cosmic flow and evolve to become fully harmonized with and resonant with the consciousness of Divine Love, Divine Give-Away. You will have to consider and study and learn what this entails. The ultimate goal is "Christ Consciousness," or "Buddha consciousness" or "God-consciousness." You may haggle over what it is called but then, that's all part of the learning.

Hassling each other over Names creates so much Grief. It's the Babble that is the Destroyer. No One has the exclusive Rights to Love, No One has the patent, the copyright, the monopoly. No One. Any who claim otherwise for their God or their religion frustrate the ultimate goal for which Humanity is destined---

to be free, creative, responsible, ever-lasting ever-loving, self-conscious citizens in a spiritual cosmos.

So Wake up! A Loving "Consciousness" is key!

*Rest assured **I Am** going to hash this all over in the next two chapters. So here is something else to put on the back burner. Let this idea simmer too--*

The delight of a lifetime awaits those who seek to personify the universal Divine Being of Love that is Themselves and Everything Else.

If everything is God, what about Evil?

God is the Darkness ...and the Light.

Sports & Video Games

Babes & Food

Got quite a brew going here, Eh?

In the meantime,
you learn by repetition.
I AM the Harper, Par Excellence.

So One more time, with vigor.

All that exists in the Universe is God.
Everything is composed of Spirit Divine.
This Means You!
There ain't nothing else!
If you think there is,
You're asleep!

Good thing You are Reading this Book!

Down through the ages, tremendous conflict has arisen over whose God is biggest and best, whose God is Diviner, whose God is

𝔱𝔥𝔢 𝔒𝔫𝔢 𝔗𝔯𝔲𝔢 𝔊𝔬𝔡,

THE ONE AND ONLY GOD.

I AM Sick and Tired of it and my patience is wearing thin. Historically, *I* have often insisted on being known as

THE ONE AND ONLY GOD

but *I AM* the God of ALL,
All-Embracing, All-Inclusive, All-Engulfing, A Singular, Unified WHOLE.
Calling Me "One and ONLY" has backfired and worked against the Divine.
The emphasis on "Only One God" degenerated into a competition of

My God is the Only God!

Not Yours! (So screw You!)

............**BUT**

I AM the One That is <u>In</u> All things.
I AM the One That <u>Is</u> the Whole.
I AM the One That is the <u>Many Parts</u>.
I AM the One Source,
the One Resource and
the One Destination.
When AnyOne Moves it is My Motion.
When AnyOne Speaks it is My Voice.
When One Thinks it is My Thought.
When ONE Dies
it is <u>MY Death</u>.
Get this through those thick skulls
that have cut you off from cosmic
consciousness! Humankind has
distorted the Original Teachings.

I BELONG TO NO ONE PEOPLE, PLACE or RELIGION!

Today, there is a popularly held sentiment that Ancient peoples who were "pantheists" <u>erroneously</u> worshipped GOD in everything.
But indeed,

I AM in All Things, I AM All Beings.

I will not deny that some degenerate Ancients got sidetracked and chose to worship MY meanest, ugliest faces, aspects or forms of ME. These denied respect to other aspects of the Whole, thus perverting their forms of worship to suit their own degenerate ends.
But LOTS of peoples are guilty of degeneration!
And in fact, sometimes One aspect of ME <u>was</u> louder, more vocal, than another. Sometimes, I did have to Choose to speak to a particular People through a particular Voice,
in the cause of spiritual evolution,
so that <u>ALL</u> may Become

Free, Responsible, Self-Conscious, Ever-loving, Ever-living Citizens in a Spiritual , (ethereal) Cosmos.

BUT in regard to Pantheism— the Ancient perception of Spirit in Everything— Truly I say to you that this is INFINITELY more respectable than that tiresome notion of
a **Far-off somewhere Mono-GOD** who , after setting
The Whole Kit and Caboodle in Motion,
has retired to the exclusive, gated community, Country Club Throne Potato Land called Heaven.

I AM NOT

some Zombie-like Virtual Reality Junkie, Peeping Tom madly watching you on my great computer monitor in the Sky, letting St. Peter do my dirty work at the gates of heaven sending poor misguided souls off to eternal damnation.
No Way Jose!
If you were an all-loving merciful God would you have the heart to send people off to eternal hell-fire? Anyway...
I AM RIGHT HERE. RIGHT BESIDE YOU, AROUND YOU, IN YOU.
EVERYWHERE.
Indeed, I AM YOU,
more than you are yourself!
I AM Both The Whole Universe and All its Potential—symbolized by the circle/zero-"O" AND I AM
the Unified Being, the Prime Existor, the Everything and the Nothing in Particular, and Every One Thing that is Unique.
WE ARE ALL TOGETHER

the Divine One and Only "1."

Allow ME to TEACH!
I Am ...of course...

☺mnipresent,

☺mniscient

&☺mnipotent

Yes Sir Ree Bob! That's what those crusty old theologians have always said that I MUST BE! And then they scratch their heads and rub their chins and try to explain just how in the universe I possiblly COULD be ☺mnipresent, ☺mniscient and ☺mnipotent...

But it's simple.

First ...To Be ☺mnipresent means That I have to be Everywhere at Once. ("Omni" means "all.")

Now as I've said in the last 79 pages... I Am the Universal Existor...I Am Everything! I Am the Ground of the Universe. I Am bikinis, hamsters, Material, Energy, Atoms, thoughts and ideas, etc. etc. etc.

So of Course....

I Am Always Everywhere at Once!!!!!

Secondly, 😊😊

--to be 😊mniscient is to know all things.

And **I KNOW** all things because
I AM the Knowing, the Mind,
the Intelligence In All Things.
Wherever there is Thought;
I AM doing the Thinking;

I Am every Thought in every Brain!

and sometimes I contradict myself!
But I Am not just Thoughts...I AM
feelings, sensations, perceptions,
awareness & emotions. Wherever there
is Perception and Consciousness--

I Am--because--you guessed it-- I Am All Things! Furthermore...I Am

The Original Eternal Chaos

and the Intelligent Order that

Creates out of Chaos.

I AM The Genius, the Order,

the Laws of Physics, the Logic,

the Wisdom, the Structural Framework,

the Matrix that underpins All Things.

I Am All Balance, Vibration, Harmony.

But be clear. ALL aspects of the
I AM, including yourselves, as well as
Beings of Spirit-- from Seraphims to devils...
are still evolving.

Some evolving parts of ME are living

in direct contradiction

to Divine Omniscience and

Divine Order and Wisdom.

Therefore, stupidity, error and Evil

exists which is unseemly, not God-like, not GOOD.

I should know, because I AM the stupid Ones *and* I AM the smart Ones!

(Indeed--it is the duty of the smart Ones, to educate the other parts of Me, so that not one be left behind.)

Alas, but for your Prophets, Saints, Christed souls and Buddhas, heros and heroines, many of you guys are but parodies, sad excuses, mockeries of your greater selves. Many are quite un-wise!
For the Human multitudes, ignorance continually creates the illusory experience of estrangement or separation from Divinity, separation from God, the Good.
But if you add up everything in the universe and realize **that that is ME**, including Past, Present and Future,
then even if parts of Me are stupid or bad, **here and now--**
in the Future--Glory Hallelujah-- this is Not to Be!
In the Future, humans will be members of the heavenly hierarchy and the Earth will be a Paradise Regained!
Therefore, in the sum total of things, Divinity Prevails... and

I AM without question

All-Knowing and Wise,
—☺mniscient!

(Even Einstein did dumb things, you know.)
And indeed, in the Future where I Am quite alive and kicking,
you guys are all awakened to supreme wisdom—
and you each have access to All My Thoughts.
(Won't You just love that!) Now...

Thirdly--

to be ☺mnipotent

is to be
All-powerful and indeed,
I AM All the
Power and Energy,
All the Potential,
All the Momentum,
All the Force that Exists
In and Around All Things.

Or to use the religious vernacular,
I AM the <u>Will (the Power)</u> of the Universe.

ALL WILL IS MY WILL.
Your Will is my Will.
Your neighbor's will is my Will.
Your enemy's will is my Will.
Your dog's will is my Will.
Etc. etc. etc.
I KNOW how things WILL turn out.
I AM how things WILL turn out.
I AM the Past, Present and Future.
I AM the Ultimate Boss.
I AM
The Power to Transform,
The Power to Remain Static,
The Power to be Bad,
The Power to be Good,
The Power to Exist.

So, I AM OKAY with "Omnipresence, Omniscience

and Omnipotence."
How about you?

Of course, I COULD hold a press conference and issue a disclaimer to say that
I AM NOT RESPONSIBLE
for all the Evil that has been done in your world; and that Lucifer, Satan, the Devil and Adolf Hitler, various sundry weirdos and despicable fanatics are
NOT My Children,
the Flesh of My Flesh.
But, paradoxically, they are!
KOOKS AND FIENDS ARE EVOLVING ASPECTS OF GOD!
Say what you will.
Bad Guys are my children.

The UnDivine is the Divine... learning how yucky

it is to be UnDivine!

In your World, Everyone is quite busy learning

"to know Good and Evil."

**Remember the Story of
"The Fall" in the Bible?
In the Bible, "The Fall" is a consequence of
the Desire "to know Good and Evil."
This is a story that represents the
launching of the Sacred and Divine Human
Exploratory Task Force from Eden.
You are <u>All</u> learning about
Badness and Goodness.
BUT**

I AM
the Alpha
and the Omega,
The Beginning
and the End.
The Buck starts
and stops with ME.
In the End, All will Come

Full Circle, And Return to Me.

This is all perfectly acceptable, right?
...Sure, and pigs can fly.
I know some of you are saying to yourselves,

"The heck with God. Who needs God anyway? This "God Is Everything" bit is as worthless as a brain fart. If God is BOTH Good and Evil... that's crazy and useless.

Furthermore...

Some of you who are Faithful Believers in ME may object to my description of who I Am on Biblical grounds or for other philosophical or theological reasons.

But first of all, please allow Me to address the Atheists and Agnostics and Cynics who are of the Modern Kind who would defer first to Science to describe what is and what is not.

My spiritual ramblings are likely just "too much" for many modern, scientifically educated, "sophisticated" thinkers.

These of My Children are quite impatient...so impatient that they are inclined to ridicule and mock the Ancient Wisdoms.

Alas it is easy to find a fault or two. And it's so much easier and convenient to go along with the same old, same old scientific model of the universe and say,

"The heck with God. Who needs God?"

So let's look at the currently popular

"scientific" view of the Universe because the fact is--

Science is Responsible (along with **ME**) for your **blind ignorance** of "THE ALL THAT IS"— OF SPIRIT DIVINE.

Because you've been brainwashed by the (so called)"Experts!" Those nerdy, socially challenged, naughty little bad boy "experts" called SCIENTISTS.

--(most scientists are the inferior male of the species)--

(OOPS..Shut your mouth Du'Tsu!...Sorry Guys, God loves you no matter what!)

<u>SCIENCE</u> pulled the wool over the eyes of 20th Century brains.

As Fyodor Dostoyevsky said in his great novel, <u>The Brothers Karamazov</u>:

...Look at the worldly and all who set themselves up above the people of God, has not God's image and His truth been distorted in them? They have science, but in science there is nothing but what is the object of sense. The spiritual world, the higher part of man's being is rejected altogether, dismissed with a sort of triumph, even with hatred. The world has proclaimed the reign of freedom, especially of late, but what do we see in this freedom of theirs?
Nothing but slavery and self-destruction....

So now it's time for a lesson on:

The Program of Scientific Materialism

Yes, 20th Century Science distorted My Image. As a result, in the "modern" world, The Flesh of My Flesh, the Creation, Spirit Divine in Manifestation is not held in high esteem and appreciated as Sacred and Divine. In fact, quite the opposite is the case because **"Scientific Materialism"** was the prevailing **THOUGHT PROGRAM** of the Twentieth Century.

Just as a computer can only function inside the parameters of its various programs, 20th Century minds were, for the most part, suckered into running on the **Program of Scientific Materialism.** This **Program of Scientific Materialism** ignores and denies the Divine. Thus human potential is severely restricted.

The current human predicament is amazingly similar to the situation portrayed in the timely film, *The Matrix*. In the film, humanity is totally unaware that it is trapped inside a complex field of illusions programmed into them by machines.

Likewise, Scientific Materialism has <u>programmed</u> humanity. It has convinced humanity that it lives in a hodge-podge cosmos that is a field of mindless, amoral forces and phenomena. Traditional religious worldviews have not kept up with science. So you are now left with a hole, a void in the soul of man. You attempt to fill this void through insatiable sensation, consumerism and consumption.

According to Scientific Materialism, God and Spirit are considered to be unnecessary and superfluous agitations when it comes to analyzing the universe. Indeed, in order to be accurate and "objective," the Twentieth Century's Scientific Materialism has tyrannically <u>demanded</u> that Divinity be totally left out of the equation, forever and ever, amen.

While pursuing science in the Twentieth Century, it was considered standard SCIENTIFIC procedure to

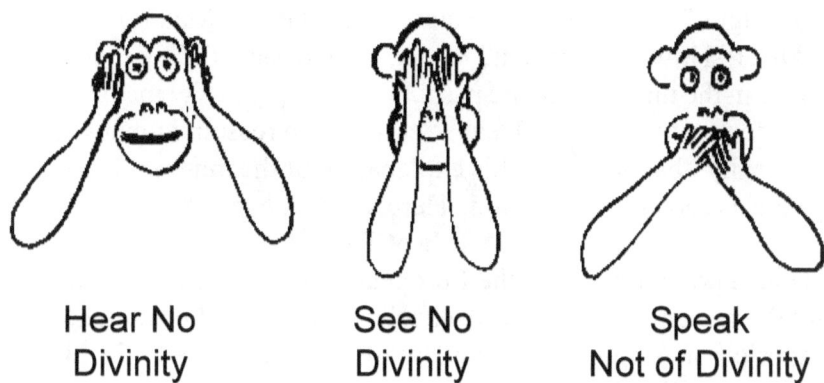

| Hear No Divinity | See No Divinity | Speak Not of Divinity |

But the era of "Scientific Materialism" must pass and a "Science of the Spirit" must replace it.

Spiritual Science must be as rigorous as any scientific discipline that exists today. Indeed, it must be **more** rigorous and **MUCH, MUCH MORE** honorable. For today, Science is manipulated by everyone with an agenda, from politicians to pharmaceutical companies and agricultural industry goliaths to those who claim to speak for Jesus Christ, among others.

You can not evolve if you throw the baby out with the bath water. The scientific method of exploring the universe is absolutely valuable. But the science that exists today is tainted and enough is enough.

Humanity is at a spiritual-evolutionary turning point. To know where you are going, you must know where you have been. You are transitioning from an essentially physical/material orientation into a multi-dimensional ethereal state of being and <u>science must help you get there.</u>

True and careful inquiry into the nature of "THE ALL THAT IS" shall lead to Enlightenment...to All-Knowingness, to "Omni-Science"

But first the grip of **The Program of Scientific Materialism** must be exorcised from human consciousness. Humanity is brainwashed, programmed. This can not be emphasized enough! You see the world "with dust in your eyes."

The booming voice of "Scientific Materialism" blasted out to 20th century mankind that "The Basic Building Blocks of all matter in the universe are "fundamental particles.'" Humans said, "That sounds about right." And you bowed down to the God of Materialism.

DUH! How smart is that? To say "the basic building block of all matter in the universe is 'the particle'" is simply to say that the whole is made up of parts! Big Deal. Yet for some reason, humankind has fanatically obsessed over this explanation of the material world as if it were a revelation from God. Here's how it happened.

A Tale of Two

Once upon a time… in the European world, the late Middle Ages and Renaissance brought forth excellent thinkers who challenged the authoritarian, dogmatic worldview of the Roman Catholic Church. The "Scientific Method" emerged as the glorious modus operandi of the "Enlightened" man. This "method" liberated the human pursuit of knowledge. Approval of the Pope was no longer considered a necessary gauge of truth. Rather, knowledge would be based on logical thinking informed by direct observation and experimentation.

The Catholic Church fought hard to maintain its grip on knowledge. In a manner of speaking, early scientists had to make a pact with the devil. So the story is told that in order to gain permission from the Pope to do dissection on cadavers, Rene Descarte, one of the fathers of modern science, agreed not to trespass into the church's realm of the mind or soul.

The Church laid claim to heaven and hell, the ethereal, otherworldly realms, the invisible, untouchable and intangible, the soul and spirit. Science staked its claim on the physical, material world, to the human body, to the earth, to the discovery of "the elements." Whatever could be studied with the five bodily senses of taste, touch, hearing, seeing and smelling fell under the jurisdiction of science.

Slowly but surely, the scientific method transformed European man's Faith in Divine Authority into a Faith in what Human Reason could explore through the five senses. Each and every human was potentially an authority, at least in regard to the earthly realm.

The natural, material world lay at the feet of Science ready to be mastered and manipulated! Why worry, scientifically, about God, the after-life, the soul, or anything "other-worldly." The "real" world-- the world of the senses--had plenty-enough challenges and rewards.

Science began as the underdog. But despite the Church's opposition, it has now won the minds and souls of man. The pendulum has swung from the Divine Authority of kings and popes to the Divine "Rightness" of Science. The hardest of hardcore "facts" is now the dominion, the royal province of Science. No knowledge of the universe is legitimate unless backed by scientific "proof" or scientific evidence.

Through the 19th and 20th centuries, scientific knowledge grew at lightning speed and pushed its way into the forefront of the modern human psyche, competing and overtaking religion as the dominant world view, or psychic "program."

However, a strange thing happened on the way to the laboratory. Originally limited to the realm of the five senses, the invention of ever more sophisticated scientific instruments--such as the electron microscope--has extended the scientific domain into the non-physical and intangible. Also, advances in higher mathematics and physics have enabled human reason to delve with great precision into highly abstract studies of time, energy, the sub-atomic (quantum) universe, and (as it is sometimes said) the "first moments of Creation."

Thus as the 20th Century came to a close, Science had ventured to explain more and more phenomena that had previously been the sole province of religion. Fields of study that had long been left to religion—for instance, the origins of life and the first moment of Creation--were no longer ignored by the scientific community. Indeed, Science has come so far as to boldly dispute and contradict various religious doctrines. The controversy over evolution is a prime example.

Paradoxically, the enigmatic science known as "quantum physics" paints a picture of reality that supports a spiritual view of the universe and humanity. However, a spiritual picture that is supported by quantum physics has not yet seeped out into the mindset of the everyday human. Not by a long shot! The majority of humans are yet deeply mired in the influence of the 20th Century's Scientific Materialism. Many profess "faith in God" but nevertheless put most of their faith in material science. Many "pooh pooh" and hold suspect the possibility of integrating spirituality and science. Many vested interests in the status quo, backed by the Spirit of Materialism, laugh all the way to the bank! Mammon, the Spirit of Greed, chuckles too.

And this is where the trouble lies.

Realize. The program of "Scientific Materialism" perpetuates the soul-numbing notion that the basic "substance" of the universe is ever more smaller parts or "particles." This program has lulled People into always looking at the Trees and never turning their view to the whole Forest. Brains running on the program of **"Scientific Materialism"** see the universe as a disjointed, patchwork quilt of pieced particles which has no over-arching Intelligence, no Unifying Principles, no harmonizing power or LOGIC governing them.

The result of this program is that your civilization is characterized by spiritual starvation, lack of respect for the Creation, and inadequate virtue. Today, **"Scientific Materialism"** has captured the collective consciousness of the world and it could be your ruin.

The particles, otherwise known as the fundamental "building blocks" of the universe, are "up for grabs," and everyone fears that there are not enough for everyone.

Consider the following. If you were to survey the ordinary, modern man or woman on a street in Hong Kong or New York City and ask him to give a description of the universe, he might start with a version of **"Scientific Materialism."** It would go something like this.

"Well, the universe we live in is made up of 'matter' and this 'matter' or material can be broken down into smaller little objects called 'atoms.' The atom has three types of particles. The center is called the nucleus and its made of positively charged particles called 'protons' and neutral particles called 'neutrons.' Swirling around the nucleus is a cloud of negatively charged particles called 'electrons.'

If our man on the street is relatively intelligent, he might go on to say, rather vaguely, that *"these particles can be broken down further into smaller parts called 'quanta' or tiny, elusive particles with many different names that can act really weird."* And he also might go on to say, *"The Universe began with a big explosion, a Big Bang and somehow, 'matter' emerged from the energies of this Big Bang, coalescing somehow into stars and galaxies and finally our solar system and planet Earth. And human life evolved from there."*

As an afterthought, the common Joe might mention a Divine Creator. But the fact is, this afterthought has little potency in day to day living because the People "give their power away" to a worldview or program that does not make the correct connections between the "building blocks" and the human Minds that think about them. That is, **The Program of Scientific Materialism** dictates that most people "see" the primary components of the universe as tiny, little pieces of material **PARTICLES that are OUTSIDE THEIR SPHERE OF INFLUENCE.**

Generally, at the <u>bottom</u> of average thinking is a picture of a singular, isolated THING called an "atom." Most likely, these atoms look like the illustration below.

Such pictures leave out so very much! These "building blocks" are not shown to be Intelligent. The pictures don't show that the atoms RESPOND to INTELLIGENCE. They do not demonstrate that they are influenced by Observation. The pictures don't show that atoms are part of a GREATER INTELLIGENT WHOLE.

Think of it! Through public education, every modern mind has been exposed to various basic pictures of the atom as the "building block" of "matter," the "stuff," of the universe.

Humanity holds an old, tired image of an Atom in its collective mind.

Generally, people imagine that the little black dots, the electrons, of an atom are circling like planets around a sun, the nucleus. They also might fill in the picture of the nucleus with protons and neutrons and break these down further into "sub-atomic" pieces.

However, a <u>more accurate picture</u> is the picture of a nucleus surrounded by a "CLOUD of POSSIBILITY" or a Cloud of Potential....where electrons may or may not be at any particular time. In fact, contemporary textbooks show an "electron cloud."

But ask yourself, "How can a picture show "POSSIBLITY?" "POSSIBLITY" speaks of something coming into existence from <u>a realm of non-existence.</u> "POTENTIAL" speaks of a non-material realm waiting to materialize. To show this, a picture must portray a non-material SEA of POTENTIAL, pregnant with a million likely and unlikely outcomes or events!

PHEW! Quite a Mind boggling notion!

Yet the collective human psyche is stuck on a static picture of an atom as a thing that is simply a complex BUILDING BLOCK.

When you think of a building block, don't you think of a hard, solid, concrete building block? You probably don't think of that concrete block as <u>MAYBE</u> being a concrete block, a POSSIBLE concrete block.

**OH HUMAN! THOU SHALT NOT THINK THAT
Atoms are like concrete building blocks--
hard and fast and real pieces of Material BEING!**

To put it simply,
Atoms are Whirlpools of
ENERGY and POSSIBILITY
within vast, wide fields or oceans
of ENERGY AND POSSIBLITY!
You and Everything else is Energy.

Some Basic Oddities

Consider these odd "facts" concerning the atom.

First-- Science says that if an atom were the size of a football field, the electrons would be the size of golf balls.

**"They" say an atom is mostly empty space
although the space is home to awesome forces.**

Science declares that electron "particles" travel around the nucleus of an atom at 600 miles per second. The protons and neutrons squeezed into the nucleus—which is 100,000 times smaller than the atom itself—whirl about in their quarters at 40,000 miles per second!

If in fact these tiny, tiny "particles" are all racing madly about inside every atom of the universe, don't you just feel like asking,

"What FORCE spurs them on?"

So I ask you--
 **Do you know what
 this is?**

**If nothing else, 20th Century minds learned about the atom's energy the hard way--by building atomic bombs.
But realize. It is not only weapons grade uranium or plutonium atoms that contain the power of the nuclear bomb.**

Every atom of "matter" holds this power, including every atom in your body. The atoms of your heart, brain, toes and belly button hold energy in a captive state. Your organs of sense— your eyes, your ears, your nose, your skin—as they are made of atoms, are **energy-filled** phenomena interacting with the similar energy-filled phenomena that make up the cosmos around you.

In the 20th Century,
humanity learned Einstein's famous equation:

$$E = mc^2$$

which means

$$Energy = Mass \times the\ Speed\ of\ Light^2$$

which Very Simply means

$$Energy = Matter$$

which means that

EVERY GOSH DARN THING IS ENERGY.

I REPEAT...

Everything Is ENERGY!

Every proton, neutron and electron is a body of energetic forces. And each particle itself DWELLS IN A FIELD OF ENERGY.

But it is not just stupid energy. It is energy which is LOGICALLY organized into atoms to give you your natural universe. It is energy governed by strict rules and laws. It is highly **RESPONSIVE, INTELLIGENT ENERGY.**

But I AM getting ahead of myself......

One need not be an Einstein to realize that indeed, the material world is really a visible manifestation of an ocean of awesome energy---a dancing, harmonious, unified field of energy!

In My humble opinion, the common scientific education has done a disservice to the minds and hearts of modern humanity. It has beguiled the People with the ring of Truth, promising to answer all questions regarding creation and the universe. But it has been like a skeleton with no flesh, no life in it, no spiritual sustenance. It has convinced humanity that it is made of "stuff" and surrounded by "stuff." You are sinking in the quicksand of this misconception. Your minds are entrapped. **Scientific Materialism** perpetuates a dangerous falsehood, a crippling myth.

Because if atoms are Energy and Potential, and NOT hard little bits of material that will never change, YOU can take control with Your Intelligence! You can be a Co-Creator with the Divine!

Modern humanity has been having a greedy, lustful, dysfunctional love affair with "particles," with "stuff." It could be a fatal obsession if it is not soon tempered. You have analyzed matter to death. You have torn everything apart, fragmented, dissected, bisected, smashed and calculated. And what have you found? In a simple yet sadly thorough sense, you found a universe made of nothing but little **bits**

and pieces of this and that. In a deeper, more complex philosophical sense, you have found Death and destruction.

You broke down atoms, gave their parts name after name; wrote your public school books and left out the most important part of the story....

Atoms are influenced by Thought and Observation. Your Beliefs create your world!

ZOWIE!

Did you ever learn that in school? Of course not.

The children of the Twentieth Century were taught that the universe is an assemblage of meek, little "building blocks" called "atoms" and even smaller "particles." They were not taught that

human thought creates reality!

Public school science worldwide has taught humans that they are "material" beings and little else. In spite of what was known and taught in advanced institutions of learning, the vast majority of average human minds were not taken beyond this scientific dogma.

After all, what has public education been but a means to create a productive workforce? With a modern education under their belt, children go out to work in factories or office, oil field or farm field, all focused on manipulating the "material" of atoms and molecules. No need to consider that you are actually an assemblage of Energy (or Divine Potential)! Wouldn't want everyone to begin to think they have real personal POWER!

The obsessive focus on understanding "material" in order to derive some practical or economic gain has mired humanity in a psychic quagmire. With frenetic fervor, the Twentieth Century science of "matter" was applied toward everything from the production of medicines and underarm deodorant to the monolithic petroleum industry and nuclear weaponry. There were and are benefits from these applications. But so very little time is devoted to looking at the big picture. Little time is devoted to the realization that true prosperity, health and material well being will only be attained when humanity discovers the secrets of its own personal, creative, <u>internal</u> energy potentials.

Now you have a tremendous amount of stuff, but unfortunately, not the "right" stuff. You have quantity but not quality. You fight wars over stuff—like oil for instance—to give you energy! Yet you are awash in energy! You are a Being composed of Energy!!!!!!!

Most fortunately, although most science was applied to economic development, nevertheless, nuclear physics and quantum physics also gave us a new picture of the universe that was extraordinary. While the common man was forced into the rat race of economic competition, in the ivy halls of pure science, physicists learned long ago what I'm trying to drill into your thick skulls here.

I want every Jack and Jill on this Earth to know that even though they now may feel and believe that they are hard, solid physical, material people, this is an illusion! I want every Jack and Jill on Earth to know that they are really Beings of Intelligent Light and Energy and Potential. 21st Century Science, especially that crazy science called "Quantum Physics," the science of the tiniest of the tiny, will help you see this.

No doubt you have heard of particle accelerators or "atom smashers." These are incredibly expensive erector sets built with government monies to split apart atoms and study their particles. So you have a civic right to know the purpose your hard tax dollars has served.

Experiments with particle accelerators prove that particles do not behave like truly solid pieces of "matter" should. When particles are smashed apart, odd "events" occur which defy "normal" physical laws.

For instance, particles can pop in and out of existence. Or particles can change, or transmute, from one kind of particle into another. This is not correct building block behavior. This is good old alchemy, the mystic's dream come true.
    "First you see lead, now you see gold!"
    But that's just one very weird thing........

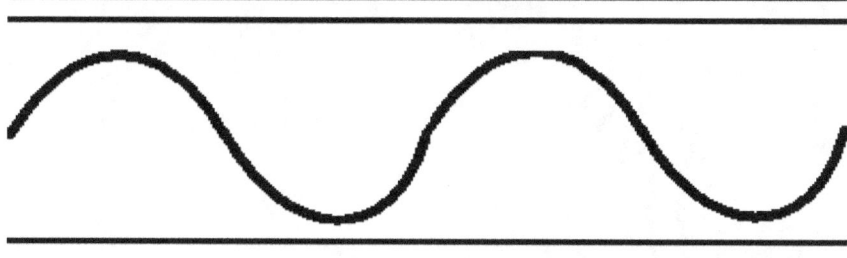

NOW LET'S TALK ABOUT WAVES!

Over and over, quantum physicists make the paradoxical statement: "Although atomic particles do act like little bits of matter just as we would expect, particles also act like waves." An electron can be recorded as a little "blip," as a point of light on a screen. But one electron can also be shot at an obstruction with two slits and go through <u>both</u> as **ONLY waves** could!

When "it" hits the target, that <u>single electron</u> makes the kind of marks that <u>waves</u> make. Such experiments prove that an electron is really a wave of "possiblity" or "potential," <u>not a solid "particle."</u>

Even more exciting, when an Observer comes onto the scene, the electron acts like a single unit again instead of waves!

In other words, it is generally accurate to say that <u>everything</u> exists as a WAVE of Energy and Potential until a human being looks at it! Then, suddenly this WAVE condenses or shrinks, or concentrates, or <u>collapses</u> into one place where the human is looking. In fact, scientists call this effect,

"The Collapse of the Wave."

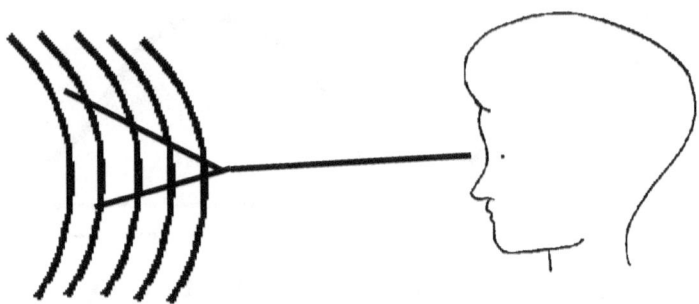

Believe it or not! A person's focus of attention, his or her BELIEF in what they are going to see-- "collapses" a wave of energy and creates "things!"

HUMANS CREATE THEIR WORLD!

The curious effect that an Observer can have on scientific experiments is not a notion that the program of Scientific Materialism finds easy to live with. After all, how much credibility can be given to the results of the "scientific method" if what you observe is actually CREATED or influenced by what you focus your attention on or by what your beliefs are, or by what your expectations are.

In other words, if scientists actually <u>influence</u> the outcome of experiments, there goes old fashioned "scientific proof" down the tube! In fact, this is a simple explanation of the high-falutin' "Heisenberg Uncertainty Principle" which states: "The path (of a particle) comes into existence only when we observe it."

But there you have it. If observations can effect and even produce "things" then obviously that's why religions can promote Faith, the energies of prayer and meditation, of thought, of consciousness. Make no mistake about it. Humans have the latent power to override the status quo of the usual everyday, so-called "material" world. Beliefs **DO** influence what happens. Miracles **CAN** be explained scientifically. But the fact is, most humans are rigidly held in very limiting beliefs of what is possible and impossible, what can be real and what can not be real.

But just you wait. Soon, everyone will be talking about how thought can influence all manner of "material objects" from plants to DNA to bodies of water (not to mention spoons.) Consider the exciting work of Dr. Masaru Emoto. He has shown through the photography of water crystals that water reacts and responds to kind words. He has shown that beautiful, well structured crystals arise when exposed to both written and spoken words of love and gratitude. Or, deformed, irregular crystals or no crystals at all form when exposed to nastiness!

Therefore, just as Neo fought to liberate humanity from the illusion called the "Matrix" you are being called to escape from the illusion of the Material, "particle" world. You are being asked to recognize that

Matter is Energy. And Energy given the name of Spirit Divine would treat you much more sweetly.

If Obie Won Kanobie was explaining all this to Luke Skywalker, he might put it this way: "Luke, the Force is With You Always. In fact, you and everything else IS the Force. And you, as a self-conscious, Intelligent being of the Force, can Master this Force."

Did you know that there is a Holy man living in India who can materialize—as if out of thin air— all manner of items such as food and jewelry, with a wave of his hand? His name is Sai Baba and his feats have been well studied, well documented and never disproved or discredited.

Realize that a true Spiritual "Master" is a Master of Energy. He or she has acquired tremendous wisdom and has learned to co-operate and co-create with the forces "behind" matter. Thank heaven, (or ME) that a primary condition for attaining this power is (usually) the development of a highly moral, ethical....indeed...a LOFTY, LOVING, Spiritual consciousness.

"Masters" of this kind do indeed walk this earth. Need I say it? Jesus the Christ knows of these masters and was a Master, among other things. Often, such Masters do not make themselves known except to the sincere and respectful seeker. They have learned to influence physical reality directly with their thoughts.

The Masters, however, do not wish to be known as miracle workers. Rather, they wish to spread a profound Knowledge of the sacred Source, Spirit Divine. They wish to share their profound Wisdoms regarding the ultimate Spiritual nature of the universe and how human consciousness is a key to the on-going Creation.

The time will come when it will be an accepted, well-known scientific premise that Consciousness plays a roll in the creation of the "material" realm. The sooner you all get with this program, the sooner happiness will be an earthly guarantee.

Scientific instruments have extended the reach of human senses into the invisible realm of energy and potential. Hence, the common man has heard a bit about nuclear radiation, ultraviolet rays, gamma rays, x-rays and so forth. But compared to human consciousness, scientific instruments are primitive and crude.

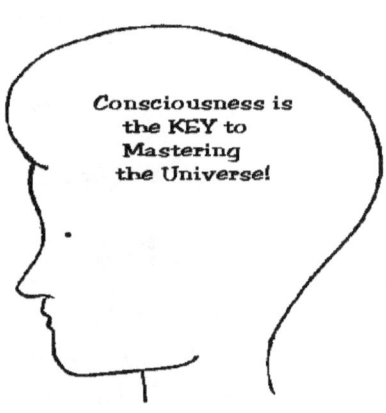

Human consciousness, when stretched to its full potential, will bestow upon humanity undreamt of success and joy. As a result of the development of consciousness, human creativity will do for the 21st century what the industrial revolution was for the last century. In fact, it will be a far more extraordinary revolution!

Therefore, I emphatically suggest that you revise your common definition of "atoms." See them not as little compact building blocks for erecting castles in a "material" world. See them rather as momentary coagulations of dancing Energy in infinite fields of Energy patterns. This is a first step to spiritual awakening.

In the meantime, tucked away in ivory towers of pure scientific research, physicists learn more and more that "matter" does not have to behave like it does for the common human. The "material" world is really a place where people could walk through walls or time travel. In fact, based upon his theories and calculations, Albert Einstein believed that time travel was possible.

Traditionally, as described earlier, ideas and talk of extraordinary human powers, of life after death and immortality have often been the province of your religious thinkers while "matter" and "energy" have been the province of science. For human destiny to be fulfilled, those of a "religious" bent and those in the "scientific" community must search for and find common ground.

A new Program of Scientific Spirituality must take root. A friendly, conscientious spiritual/scientific dialogue must transpire within the modern context of sophisticated scientific understanding. And sure enough, the ancient Wisdom that has always said that the Universe is the Sacred Divine One will be verified. Faith will be supported by knowledge.

Human destiny demands a marriage between scientific knowledge and spiritual wisdom, ethics, honor and reverence.

The Times Inquirer

SOCIAL SHOCKER!
Si Enz, Ima Spirit tie the Knot

Odd Couple Agrees to Agree

Cosmos--Odd couple, Si Enz and Ima Spirit, were wed Thursday evening in a service held by a babbling brook in a forest clearing. The multitudes were in attendance.

The bride, dressed in an ethereal silk tafetta gown of radiant energy by God is My Source Designs, beamed happily when her betrothed agreed to recognize her as a legitimate approach to reality and pledged to be always honorable. The new Mrs. Spirit-Enz vowed in her turn not to flirt too much with pseudo-science, be too bitchy, self-righteous, superstitious or "la-la-esque."

In their vows, the couple asserted that their Reverence, Piety and Faith would be based on Knowledge...OmniScience.

Yes! Spirit Divine lurks in the shadows awaiting your scientific thinking, awaiting a legitimacy based on rigorously clear intelligence. Spirit Divine hovers in the wings of the Future. The era of the **New Atom, the Spiritualized Adam**, waits upon the decision of free thinking, creative humans.

One can see it coming. Thank **ME**. There is more and more of a trend these days for spiritually open scientists and scientifically trained writers to address the question of where Spirit or at least the "miraculous" fit into the current more sophisticated scientific models of the universe.

Just to name a few, take for example Michael Talbot's <u>The Holographic Universe</u>; Bruce Lipton's, <u>The Biology of Belief</u>; and Fritjof Capra's <u>The Tao of Physics</u>. Films such as *What the Bleep Do We Know*, *Indigo* and *The Matrix* assist in Spiritual Scientific awakening. (The media need to do their share too.)

Quantum and relativity theory, particle physics, higher mathematics, string theories and holographics CAN be simplified for mass public communications. To fit God or Divinity into the same picture, these disciplines can be used to "prove" that miracles are not irrational impossibilities. They can provide a context for understanding what has been defined as "the supernatural." Hithertofore, **"scientific materialism"** has been used to explain *away* "spiritual" phenomena. It is time for the pendulum to swing back in the direction of the scientific *affirmation* of miraculous and awesome possibilities.

On the surface, it may seem that comparatively little profit lies in teaching a difficult subject when average Joes and Josephines can produce new, improved underarm deodorant and play computer games without knowledge of quantum mechanics, not to mention without knowledge of God. Indeed, certain worldly powers do not wish the common People to be empowered. But....

A crossroads looms ahead. It is time to decide.

I have not minded that I, Spirit Divine, have been left totally out of your popular science textbooks and studies in public schools. **Your freedom to choose is excruciatingly important and I must work with respect toward this freedom.** And the difficulties of life today--the isolation, the loneliness, financial worries, the desperation in the face of disease and hunger and calamity—even the violence and deprivation—is the breeding ground from which a great spiritual leap forward will be made--the ashes from whence the Phoenix rises!

Science's neglect, indeed, its dismissal of Spirit was necessary. It creates a new route for a return to the ONE and is a part of modernity's destiny. (Many other old belief systems had gotten way out of hand.) The modern world is now a breeding ground for True Seekers of clear intelligence and for the evolution of a spiritual wisdom enhanced by science.

"Salvation is by Faith alone!" cry so many religious believers. Don't worry about using a hard-core, robust science to consider spiritual realities! Knowledge is knowledge. Faith is faith and never the twain shall meet!

"HECK NO!" says Spirit Divine. It's Time for a Science of the Spirit! Drag those pure thinkers out of their ivory towers and force them to tell you the Truth...that science SUPPORTS the existence of so-called "miracles." Your illnesses CAN be healed with the energy of thought and meditation! You can live on the sunlight!

OF COURSE...I never intended to simply reveal Myself under an electron microscope or through a telescope to just anyone. In every Age, only True Seekers find **ME**.

So many are ready to be True Seekers!

You have reached an era when many are ready to understand and a time for the balance in the use of your science has arrived. The modern mind must awaken to the view that the universe is a field of energy where ethereal--not "material" Beings of Intelligence play.

The general public must be given a revised version of "the rest of the story" in understandable terms. In the very least, they must be shown how science need not contradict or disprove "spiritual" claims.

Skeptics often label the use of science to support spiritual views as "pseudo-science," particularly when such science is not rigorously pursued with intellectual integrity. Some such skepticism can be healthy but scathing ridicule is not. Humans tend to be gullible and easily exploited. But worse than gullibility is arrogance and censure.

History often has shown that nay-sayers and pontificators must eat their words in the end. The label, "pseudo-science" is too frequently the tool of control freaks who, having appointed themselves to be "watchdogs," become ravenous, rabid wolves.

Always there is the need for tolerance and patience, open-mindedness and appreciation for kind-spirited dialogue.

In the final analysis, the Human Spirit longs not only for Faith but for Knowledge as well. Such a thirst will and must be quenched. Your destiny is Omni-Science, the Knowledge of the All! Scientists must assist in plumbing the depths of the bottomless Spiritual well that is this Universe in a manner that feeds the Soul, not just the body.

Indeed...All People---from the most sophisticated physicist to the hill billy in the hollow---have their own eyes to see. Each can read the spiritual script wherever they might look. My messages are written in the language of symbols. And I have, in a manner of speaking, a very prominent "logo." **I**, Spirit Divine, bear witness to My awesome Presence by weaving My initial into the spiraling of galaxies, from whence the ancients devised the letter "G" for God or Genesis.

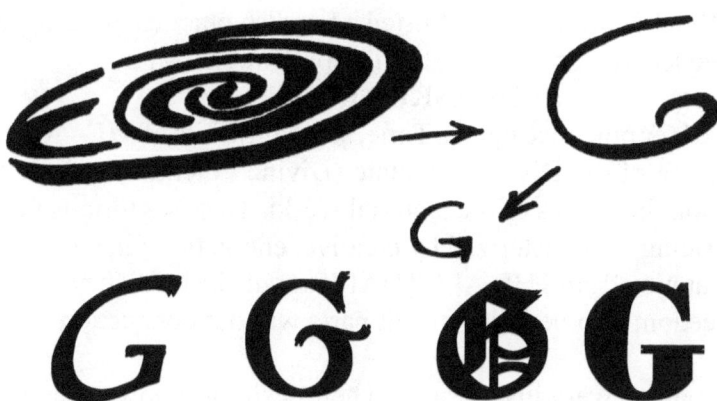

The spiraling, of course, is a phenomenon that is both Circular and Wave-like in its essential nature. And need I remind you that at the core of your human **GENES**, there lies the circling, spiraling double helix of the DNA. This is no coincidence. This is evidence of the Intelligence, the Knowing, that works in You and Through You.

My intelligence is manifest in the spiraling whirlpool and the vortex of the hurricane or tornado. Where **AM I NOT** evidencing Myself? Look to the snail's shell. The spiral is one of my signatures, My Logos, My Word, My Symbol, My Expression.

When atom smashing scientists manage to discover yet another "fundamental particle," pat themselves on the back and talk about the ultimate "building blocks" of the universe, take it as a grain of salt. It is only a piece of the cosmic cinnamon bun they are ruminating upon. When they demonstrate God's existence with a Unified Field Theory of Divine Love, that will be Nobel Prize-worthy.

You, as a human being, are a Divinely Intelligent holographic projection of energy upon the 3 Dimensional cinematic screen of an inaccurately titled flick called "The Material World." And **I AM** all the actors and actresses, all the props, all the heroes, all the villains, all the kings and all the presidents. It can be no other way.

Truly, I say unto you...The "reality" of the material world as "material" is a sleight of hand trick! I AM a first rate illusionist, not only the Prime Mover but the Prime Prestidigitator, a magician extraordinaire! Now you see it, now you don't! I play a wily coyote with you and Myself.

Yes. **I** confess. **I** have foisted a fiendish practical joke on you all. **I** have led you down the path of error. But the fact is,
YOU ASKED FOR IT!
Believe it or not, once upon a Time, some little bits of **ME**—waves from the sea of the Divine Potentate (Divine Potential)—chose to FALL upon the shores of the material world. That is, glorious faces of **ME**, Beings characterized by creative, energetic will, wondered what separation from THE ALL THAT IS would be like. They wanted to try freedom—to be independent parts without connection to the whole.

These beings were just curious. Their desire to know separation was not Evil—misguided perhaps--but not unforgivably damnable. Ask and ye shall receive. That is the Sacred way of Creation. Their wish was MY COMMAND. My nature is to Give. Alas, they asked for what was not offered...and I gave it anyway.

I created your world of ignorance and stupidity because how else can you learn? To paraphrase the Bible, these "**I AM'S**"—these parts of **ME**—hungered to eat of the fruit of the tree of the knowledge of good and evil—to be know-it-alls like **ME**, (the fancy word is "Omniscient.") Therefore, **I** cast a veil of illusion over these Beings, a veil that separated them off from cosmic vibrations...Universal Harmony. **I** planted seeds of consciousness in fields of darkness where they could eventually blossom with the fruit of self-illumination.

I encased the **"I AM," parts of MYSELF, THE CREATOR,** in soft mushy brains inside the hardest of minerals, the skull, cutting their thoughts off from cosmic consciousness. I gave them their little <u>individual</u> selves, their particular identities.

**Your Brain is now trapped in your Skull!
In the normal course of events, only the innocent babe, the infant with an open fontanel (the soft spot) is in direct contact with Spirit worlds! As it grows shut, unless you strive to reconnect, your skull runs interference with the vibrational frequencies of Spirit Divine. But the Spiritual Master tunes in.... becomes again as a child and is "Enlightened," and "Knows All..."
.........becomes..........."Omniscient!"**

The profound gift of human self-consciousness has evolved through the choice of these "**I AM'S**." But alas, so has egotism, selfishness, tyranny and fear.

I gave D(A)TH to these facets of Myself to further cut them off from what is Real and Eternal. The security that accompanies eternal suckling at the breast of Spirit Divine was denied. Thus was implanted the desire to seek and reunite with the Holy Spirit, yea, even the Spirit of Truth, the Divine Word. (More on these later.) Only those who dare to seek, challenging appearances and convention, practicing spiritual arts, receive the milk and honey of Divine Illumination. But Grace is available to all.

In asking for separation, **WE** were playing with the impossible! There can be no Real Separation from **Me** because **I AM THE ALL THAT IS. Each little seed was a piece of ME, a seeming "particle," but really inseparable from the Whole, the One!**

Today You feel yourself to be a Single Unit, a unique "I Am," -- a little One within the whole One, within the Greater Divine Whole that is the One Universe. Merge with me and be Free! You are one of God's Eyes, God's "I's."!

For the sake of cosmic evolution, for the sake of the acquisition of Self-Knowledge, **WE** devised a place called "The Material World." Here, human Beings could have, if you will, a "virtual" experience of Separation. It was a mutual agreement between Me and Thee, for we are One. And there should be no eternal blame assigned for this wish to extend the boundaries of knowledge.

What of Satan, The Serpent, Eve's big blunder, The Temptation and the Fall?

Satan be vanquished! He must fade into the mists of time. He is an over-simplified caricature of evil whose Time has run its course. To assign responsibility for Evil to the Devil rather than to pure human error and design is to deny yourself power! If Satan is seen as an ugly and outmoded aspect of the Divine-Self that is YOUR SELF then humans will be in control and Satan can be "cast out."

Furthermore, the Snake's role in the Biblical account of the Fall has too long been misunderstood. In the Eastern traditions of spirituality, the Snake symbolizes Creative, life-giving energy known as the Kundalini that is a vital part of every human. Of course this kind of energy can be abused. But to master it is to master the self!

Consider the Caduceus. The symbol of the medical profession that was carried by the Greek god of healing, Mercury, represents this same kundalini energy, the Creative energy. So it's time to give a little slack to the Snake!

And poor, poor Eve! How could she not resist the lure to Creativity, the Serpant's temptation? She is the "Womb"- man, woman, the Man with the WOMB, the organ which creates the human child. Her nature is to create!

Further, **the Feminine aspect of God is Wisdom.** I Will speak of this in a later chapter. Put that on the Back Burner.

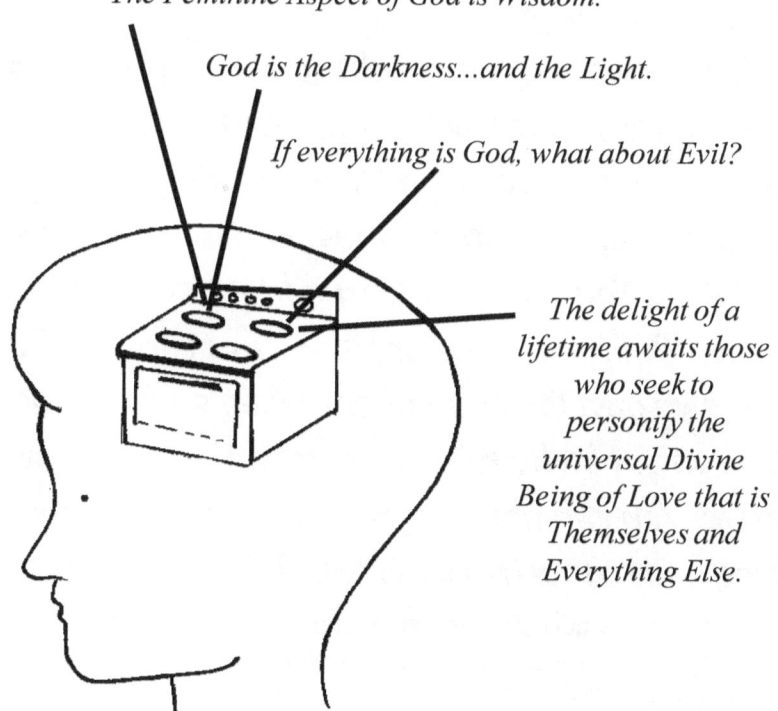

The Feminine Aspect of God is Wisdom.

God is the Darkness...and the Light.

If everything is God, what about Evil?

The delight of a lifetime awaits those who seek to personify the universal Divine Being of Love that is Themselves and Everything Else.

WE, the Divine You and I, are nearing the ultimate goal. You have learned the lessons of freedom. Many of you know or are on the verge of realizing that

SEPARATION FROM GOD STINKS!

So not to worry. The illusions of the materiality to which you still cling will fade. The Time will come when you will know yourselves to be ethereal beings of Light energies and One with Spirit Divine, for as I said, in spite of yourselves, you always HAVE BEEN, you always ARE and you always WILL BE Spirit Divine.

You and I are of the same Substance—Spirit Divine.

If you don't believe you are Spirit Divine, it's no wonder. You have been taught so very little. You are just a massive clump of little ole atomic particles, right?

You have not been taught to walk through walls or on water. You have not learned to heal with a touch or to produce food from thin air. You can not see other-dimensional beings, fairies and angels or Buddhas. You have not learned to fast for days on end or to live on the sunshine. You can not "see" your own past life or another person's rainbow aura. You can not invite rain to a parched land and have it arrive. You can not live 5000 years. But this sort of thing and so much more is ABSOLUTELY POSSIBLE.

Don't believe Madonna—the rock star, that is. You are not just a material girl or boy living in a material world. You are a Being of Divine Spirit Energy.

Chapter on The One--Review

The Whole Entire Universe is
Spirit Divine,
the Ground of the Whole World, The Divine Will-Energy and Potential, It is All The Divine
One!
Spirit Divine Shouts from every corner of the Universe but only True Seekers have ears to Hear the Words..."I Am."

The Rift between
Science and Spiritual Wisdom
must be healed.

Seek the knowledge that will heal you!

$$0=1=0=1=0=1=0=1=0$$

The All equals
The One which equals The All...
Forever and Ever.

Yea So Be It...AMEN.

As long as you remain in one extreme or the other, You will never know oneness.

The Great Way by Sengstan
(Third Zen patriarch)
Translated from the Chinese by Richard Clark

Therefore become perfect, just as your
Father in Heaven is perfect.

Matthew 5:48

So's your Mother ...

E.G.M.Richie

The Two

This one and only begotten world has become the God perceptible to the senses, and the greatest and best world, the fairest and most perfect there could be.

From <u>The Timaeus</u>...Plato

"The Cosmic Powers have no inexhaustible reservoir of Light. Their reservoir is one from which the stream of forces will constantly diminish unless from human life itself, through efforts to transform thinking, feeling and willing to rise into the higher worlds, fresh forces, new light were to flow back into the great reservoir of Cosmic Light and Cosmic Feeling. We are now living in the epoch where it is essential for humankind to be conscious that we must not merely rely upon what flows into us from Cosmic Powers, but must ourselves be coworkers in the process of world evolution."

Rudolf Steiner, <u>Macrocosm and Microcosm,</u>
Lecture IV,   March 23, 1910.

The Dance

Run Away! Run Away!

En Garde! Put up your dukes! Prepare for combat!
Let's fight. Let's argue. Let's get mean. Let's be nasty. Let's
spit on each other with self-righteous slobber. Let's insult
each other's integrity and honor, intelligence and humanity.
Let's play dirty. Let's sling mud. Let's laugh in each other's
faces. Let's be sooo condescending, smug and sarcastic.
Let's smirk through our holier-than-thou know-it-all teeth
and hyperventilate with intolerance. Let's stick bodkins in
each other. Let's glare at each other with voo-doo pins and
needles. Let's silently fume and eat out our insides over
each other's stinking, nauseating

Inferiority, Ignorance and Evil.

Let's thank heaven we are going there and "They" are not!
Let's shiver coldly at the thought
that just maybe our adversary is
possessed by the Devil or <u>IS</u> the Devil Himself!

They're Evil! Run Away! Run Away!
Well,...Lets just Nuke each other once and for all..
OR you can simply listen to
ME!

Pretty please with a cherry on top. Thank you very much.
Sigh. Such a stiff necked people!
Just consider one touchy subject:

"CREATION VERSUS EVOLUTION"

The Whole Controversy is SO Tiresome. After All,

The Past and Future Do Not Exist!
??????????

They don't? Well Golly Gee, God, if there ain't no past, then there tweren't no Creation and couldn't never been no Evolution neither!!!!!
Now, please stop and think.
What I AM saying is that

THE PAST AND THE FUTURE ARE PHYSICALLY UNMANIFEST.

You can not "Sense" the past and future with any of your physical senses.
You can not touch last month's spaghetti dinner with your fingertips
or taste next week's spaghetti with your tongue.
Past and Future are way beyond the reach of
IMMEDIATE BODILY SENSATION. SOOOO,
WHERE CAN YOU FIND THE PAST & FUTURE?

NOWHERE

within physically manifest experience. The Past and Future are **Not** part of what you call "The Material World!" (Duh!)
Normal bodily, physical sensation can bear witness only to the fleeting "Material" EVENT called "NOW."
I have said that there is no material world.
The "NOW" is a focus of energy, a concentrated, sensibly perceptible, spiritual event.
Now hear this: The Past and Future are part of

The Ineffable Darkness,
The Hidden,
The Great Mystery.

They are non-physical and immaterial,
(at least as far as normal human perception and experience are concerned).

I REPEAT.

Your connection to the Past and Future does not occur in the realm of physical, bodily sensation.
So what's the big deal? So what if you can't touch, hear, taste, smell or see the Past and Future?
Well...How can you possibly

𝕭𝖊𝖑𝖎𝖊𝖛𝖊 𝕴𝖓

anything that you can't touch, taste, feel, smell, hear or see?
How can you possibly
BELIEVE IN the PAST AND FUTURE?
What proof do you have of their existence?
Go to the refrigerator and find last year'spaghetti that you have already eaten. Is the spaghetti that you have eaten still in the refrigerator?

NO! NO! NO!

Where is that spaghetti? ... It has Transformed!
A minute on the lips, a year on the hips.
It has disappeared and transformed.
It has Metamorphosed.

YES! YES! YES!

The actual spaghetti that Once Was, Is No More.
It has passed into oblivion. It No Longer Exists!
Although you can see it with your Mind's eye,
You can not hear, taste, touch, feel or smell it.
It's LOOOONG GONE.

SO........THE POINT IS:
Your connection to the Past and Future
does not occur in the realm of bodily sensation.
You can not taste, touch, hear, see or smell
The Past or Future.

So, why Am I harping on this?

Realize: You Know the Past and Future not

through your senses but through your Mind!

You know the past and future with solely, only and exclusively your mind, your thoughts, your intelligence, your reason, your inner vision, your logic, your memory, your imagination, your mental faculties,
OR -to sum all these up—
WITH the POWERS OF

CONSCIOUSNESS.

Only through the power of <u>Super-Sensible Consciousness</u>, are you aware that the Past and Future Exist.

You can remember last year's spaghetti.
You can imagine tomorrow's feast.
So obviously, Memories go <u>above</u> and <u>beyond</u> Bodily/Sensible consciousness. They are "super-sensible."

Therefore, in the following discussion I will always refer to "Bodily Consciousness" when I Am speaking of immediate sensory experience. However, for most of the following discussion, when using the term "consciousness," it will refer to consciousness that does not rely upon the bodily senses. Rather, it consists of mental or psychic phenomena such as ideas, mental images, memories, thoughts, emotions and intuition. These may be triggered by or rely on experiences of bodily sensations but they do not have to be.

TRUE Bodily Consciousness
gives you the experience of

The Now.

Super-sensible consciousness can give you as a human being, an experience of something that lies outside the fleeting flow of the moment.
Wisdom and Logical thinking
take you "outside" the body.

For instance, imagine a triangle, a geometrical figure with three straight sides connected with three angles.

Pythagoras discovered all sorts of exotic rules about triangles, including his famous theorem. $a^2 + b^2 = c^2$

Where did these rules come from?

The Realm Beyond the Senses!
The "Other-World"

A triangle does not depend on the immediate sensory world for verification. That is to say, only a triangle can be a triangle because it is a thing which exists by virtue of a rule, a code, a formula, or in other words, by mathematical principles. The rules of triangularity do not depend on the physical world for existence. *Rather, the rules hover in the nether realm of the non-physical, waiting for super-sensible consciousness to grasp it.*

The rules exist whether you or any other human are around to think about them or not.

"Well," you say, "the idea of the triangle needs my mind to exist, and my mind needs my body, doesn't it?"
Actually.....No it doesn't...

But this is missing the point.
The point is that the IDEA OF THE TRIANGLE existed before your mind existed and before the Mind of Pythagoras. THE IDEA OF THE TRIANGLE exists both in a realm of past experience and in a realm of future potential. It dwells eternally in the universe somewhere, <u>waiting for Minds to grasp it</u>.

The Principle or Rule of Triangularity exists in TIME outside the NOW.

This simple Idea of the Triangle bears witness to a whole category of INTELLIGENT eternal phenomena that "live" and have their being outside the world of the manifest, outside the realm of the physical. The rule of the triangle is evidence of a realm of "higher existence" that usually is experienced only by thinking, intelligent Consicousness. It bears witness to a realm of Truth and Principles. It bears witness to a living field of Wisdom.

Note that when consciousness grasps the idea of a triangle, the mathematical rules which apply to it can not be altered or broken by human thinking. The principles relating to triangles are fixed and lasting in duration. They may require a medium for their expression in this world--paper and pencil, for instance—but they do not require a paper and pencil or any other physical thing in the NOW for their existence.

The RULE OF TRIANGLES LIVES IN the REALM of ETERNITY.

These rules or PRINCIPLES are independent of existence in the NOW, free from the slings and arrows of outrageous physical manifestation and human sabotage.

The Principles are Eternal.
The Symbols are Eternal.

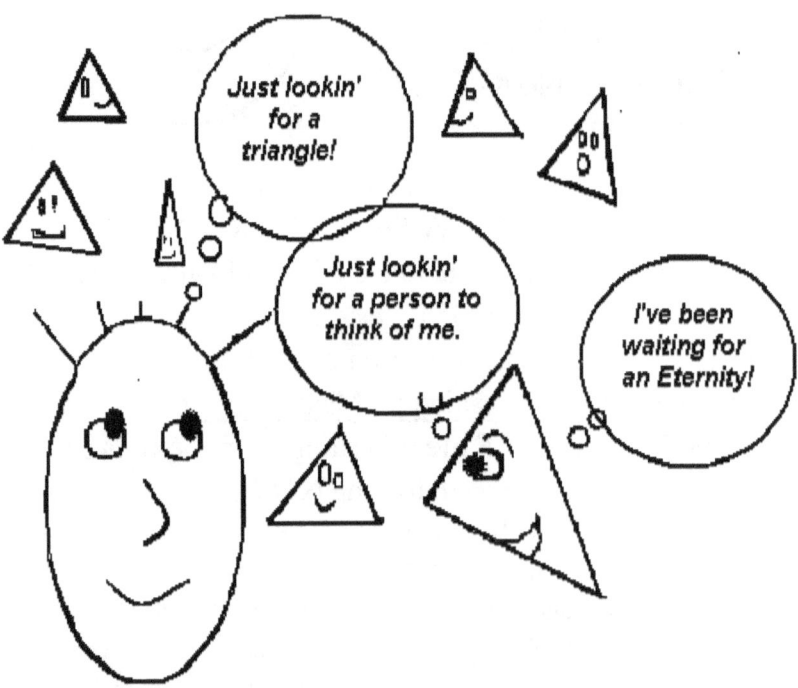

A triangle in the fifth century was the same as a triangle in 1953. A triangle is the same in any nation on earth and can be the same in every human mind. Triangles are free for everyone!

The idea of Triangles lives in the realm of "universal truth."

These ideas transcend 3-dimensional space.

At one time you learned about a triangle—in the past. Now as you think of it, you are dealing solely with a **Super-Sensible** notion having nothing to do with what you are physically tasting, eating, smelling, touching or hearing.

Ideas of triangles, as it were, float in the sea of Universal Ideas, Past and Future—as an Ideal—waiting to be fished out by inquiring minds.

Ideas "pop" into your head. Where do they come from?

Your physical brain serves up the idea to you.

But the idea, once learned, connects you with a universal reality that is independent of your brain or body.

The Idea of the triangle comes from a place outside of Time where the universal principles of triangles

hang out.

The law of triangularity reverberates eternally.
Your mind recognizes this reverberation.
You say, "Aha! I know what a Triangle is!"
And EVERYONE AGREES!
The things that humans call Ideals, Universal Truths,
Laws and Principles are maintained
Outside of the Fleeting world of the Moment.

When the Mind grasps at Truth, it is reaching for something which extends itself through All of Time. And when the Mind reaches, It often finds.

Super-sensible consciousness gives the human being access to the realm beyond the present moment.

Consciousness Connects Humanity to Eternity.

Consciousness
connects the human being to the place where Intelligent, Eternal Ideals Dwell—
Ideals and Principles
LIVE in a manner,
totally unlike Human Life.
Ideals and Principles and Beings
that Embody Ideals (<u>YES Beings!</u>)
Live Unchanging and Undying,
In the Realm of Spirit.

Logic and understanding and noble feelings are like a doorway into the non-material realm, the realm of Intelligent Being- Energies. Ideas, reason, wisdom, logic, imagination, intuition, understanding and the light of knowledge connect humans to

non-physical/Spiritual worlds.

Thinking can stretch your Being beyond the boundaries of your skin, and the sky is not the limit!
Therefore, the Realm of
Thinking, Feeling and Willing,
The Realm of Super-Sensible Consciousness,
Is The Ultimate Frontier,
The Place for 21st Century Pioneers.

Consider Your Memories.
These are Verifications of the Past.
Consider Your Hopes and Dreams, Prayers and Plans.
These are Patterns for the Future.
All occur within the Province of
Super-Sensible Consciousness.

Again, Your Bodily Consciousness can give the verification of the existence of things in the NOW—through bodily senses.

But Your Consciousness can also give verification of things beyond the NOW, existing in the NON-PHYSICAL...Spirit Realm.
Consciousness Verifies The Existence of Realms Outside the Physical.

???????????????????????????????

Does your darkened mind resist the notion that

ETERNAL THINGS CAN EXIST?

Perhaps THE PAST AND FUTURE
and TRIANGLES are mere
conjurings of the physical brain?
Perhaps Ideas about such things are
bio-chemical hallucinations?!!!

MERE DELUSIONS?

Is the brain having the last laugh on humans by constantly fooling them into believing that there is anything beyond the immediate boundaries of their physical senses?
Is the physical brain churning out thoughts that are just a random jumble of biochemical processes
in a random accidental universe
of molecules, atoms, and particles?

Is there a past and future?
Ha Ha Ha Ha Ha. How can anyone believe that the Past and Future Exist?
HA HA HA HA HA!

WHAT ARE YOU WILLING TO BELIEVE EXISTS?

ARE YOU SO AWESOMELY WISE AS TO HAVE FAITH IN THE NON-PHYSICAL, IMMATERIAL, IMPERCEPTIBLE

PAST AND FUTURE?

Will tomorrow come? Did yesterday happen?
If you choose to Believe In Yesterday and Tomorrow, even though they don't physically exist in the NOW,

Glory Halleluyah!!

Your mind is embracing, grasping, clinging to the
Ideal, the Rule, the Principle of the Passage of Time,
You depend on the
POTENTIAL AND POSSIBILITY
Of MATERIAL EXISTENCE
and that the universe will continue to abide by the rules
it has for eons been committed to.
Your Ears Cannot hear the Voices of the Past.
Your Eyes Cannot see the Sights of the Future.
Your Tongue Cannot Taste the Foods of the Ancients.
Your Fingers Cannot Feel the Warmth of Your Ancestors.
Your Nose Cannot Delight in the Scent of the Flowers
of 2012 AD.
**BUT…Can you not see that
THE PAST AND FUTURE—
which do not exist physically—**

ARE SPIRIT DIVINE?

THE MATERIAL CREATION—**THE NOW**—IS
DIVINE SPIRIT THAT CAN BE PERCEIVED BY
THE FIVE SENSES--AND

The Material Creation is Re-Created

Every New Moment
AND IS EVOLVING
ETERNALLY!

You and everything else is a dynamic field of
Dancing Energies
that continually
enters into Being
from the invisible realm of Spirit
and in turn disappears
into the invisible body of Spirit.

Comprende vous?

Each fleeting instant....

is created and destroyed.

There is...

CONSTANT CREATION

and

ETERNAL EVOLUTION.

The material realm or physical reality is characterized by

Eternal Change, Eternal Transformation,
Eternal Transmutation, Eternal Metamorphosis,
Eternal Transfiguration, Eternal Shapeshifting.
Eternal Birthing. Eternal Rebirthing.
The REALM OF HUMAN EXISTENCE is like some giant magnetic vacuum cleaner sucking up Energy/Spirit from the unmanifest past and future and funneling and focusing and compacting it into the reality called "The Present," or, as pundits and sages have called it, the

"ETERNAL NOW"

THE "NOW" DRAWS ITS SUSTENANCE FROM THE PAST AND FUTURE, AND FROM THE DARK AND FIREY GOLDEN REALM OF POTENTIAL AND IDEALS.

Your earthly material world is a highly concentrated focus of Spirit/Energy. The bodily sense organs acquaint you with the Spirit which exists in the realm of the physical present, in the moment called

"NOW," WHERE ALL IS OF MORE OR LESS FLEETING DURATION.

However, your wondrous, magnificent mental processes within your consciousness can connect you with the Spirit Realm

Outside Time,

where ALL is characterized by

EXTENDED DURATION.

The Realm Outside Time is a Spirit Realm called 'Eternity.'

It is as real as the nose on your material face.

It is Absolute Potential.

It holds the Wisdom of the Ages, the Hope of the Future.
Beings, events and phenomena in the eternal realm
endure over tremendous expanses of TIME.
Even if you are as dumb as a doornail, you can still have a vague idea of yesterday's birthday party and tomorrow's football game. If you let your imagination go wild, you can probably envision billions of years of endless time with planets revolving around suns and stars whirling through the galaxies. Your mind, your mental musings, <u>your</u> supersensible <u>consciousness</u>, can transport you into this "heavenly realm" of incredibly long duration.
The real trick is to appreciate the following facts regarding

Your Consciousness:
IT CAN REACH BEYOND
DEATH!!!!!!

YOUR CONSCIOUSNESS KNOWS NO TIME LIMITS, NO PHYSICAL LIMITS, NO BOUNDARIES.

Can you believe it?
Put "The Limitless Possibilities of Consciousness"
on the back burner along with...

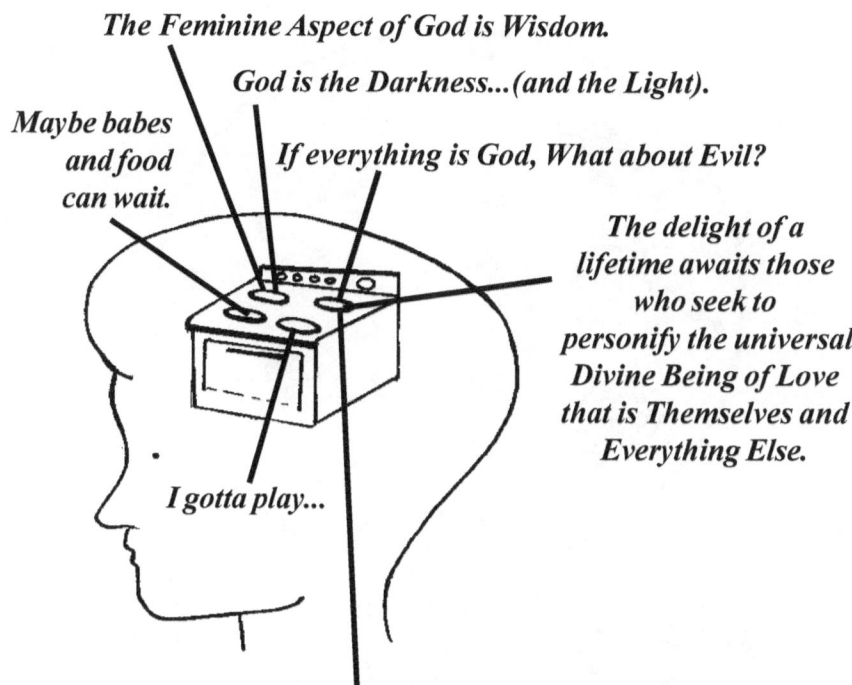

Meanwhile, at the risk of being redundant, recall that I have told you,

I AM

"THE ALL THAT IS" and so I Am PHYSICAL AND NON-PHYSICAL, MANIFEST AND UNMANIFEST, MATERIAL AND IMMATERIAL.

I AM THE <u>ONE</u>, Spirit Divine.

I AM

THE WHOLE KIT AND CABOODLE.

THE VISIBLE PART OF ME IS CALLED THE "PRESENT,"
THE NOW.
TWO of MY INVISIBLE PARTS ARE CALLED
"PAST" AND "FUTURE."
FOR HUMANS ON EARTH, THE MATERIAL CREATION ETERNALLY
IS BOTH CREATED AND RE-CREATED.
IN EACH FLEETING INSTANT OF EXPERIENCE IN TIME,
THERE IS BEGINNING AND ENDING AND ANOTHER BEGINNING.
SO THERE IS ETERNAL CHANGE,
TRANSMUTATION, TRANSMUTATION, TRANSFIGURATION,
OR, IF YOU WILL,
<u>EVOLUTION</u>, FROM EVERY FLEETING MOMENT TO THE NEXT.

The Divine Creation is Ongoing and Endless.

To say something like:
"In the Beginning God created..."
IS POSSIBLY MISLEADING BECAUSE
I never stopped.

I AM still Beginning!

I did not turn the Universe, the earth and its inhabitants on like some ancient VCR and then sit back to be some Grandfatherly Finger Wagging Nag in the Sky—
with no possibility or hope of changing the tape.

I GIVE MY FLESH

MOMENT BY MOMENT TO YOU AND TO YOUR WORLD.

Like the Sun itself,
Spirit Divine rays into the NOW from
the Past and Future.

In Every Moment of Ongoing Beginning
I SAY: Let there be Light!

Particles (OR ENERGY) emerge and harmonically converge
into the NOW as colorful atoms from
Out of the Ineffable Darkness of Potential
into the physical world.

THE BIG BANG NEVER CEASES, NEVER CEASED, NEVER WILL CEASE.

*All "Material" Creation constantly explodes out of the Darkness as Light and Form.
All the Creation which you sense with your bodily senses, in its multiplicity of forms and shapes is Born Out of Eternity into the NOW.*

And of course......I AM Both the NOW <u>and</u> Eternity.
The Greeks had a name for a God, Titan, that existed before
the Birth of their better known gods.
That Titan was called Chronos......or in a Word, TIME.

I AM that invisible GOD, I Am Time... "CHRONOS." I AM the Ancient of Days, Alpha and Omega. the Grand Mother and Grand Father of the Creation.

The Creation is Both My Grand Child, and My Beloved Child.

THE CREATION IS THE FLESH OF MY FLESH

THIS SENSATIONAL EVENT WHICH OCCURS AT THE
CROSSROADS
OF THE PAST AND FUTURE
IS THE CHILD OF HIDDEN, DIVINE
SPIRITUAL Forebears,

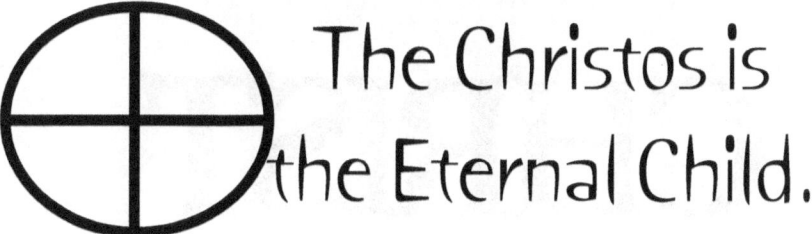

The Christos is the Eternal Child.

THIS OFFSPRING called THE NOW,
this Child that is your Universe--
is Born Out of Eternity from the Cross-Breeding---
the Uniting of the I AM, the Existor,
the Father Will-to-Be
with the Untainted Virginal Mother Wisdom
which consists of Pure Principless and Eternal Truth.

THE PHYSICAL WORLD IS BORN WHEN
THE PAST,
THE SEEDS OF BEING,
OF WILL, OF POWER AND POTENTIAL
UNITE WITH WHAT IS TO COME,
WITH WISDOM, THE FUTURE,
THE ETERNAL IDEALS OF THE GODHEAD.

YOU CAN CALL MY CHILD,
The NOW or

"YOUR REALITY"

TRULY I SAY UNTO YOU:
The Now Itself is the

LIVING CHRIST

MY FIRST BORN, THE ONE BEGOTTEN.

THE CHRISTOS IS BORN FROM THE COUPLING OF THE WIDSOM AND THE WILL OF THE UNIVERSE.

I Am the Father-God,
The Will-To-Be,
the Ground of the World,
The Body of the All, the
Existor, Creator,
the Masculine
Aspect of God.

I bear the seeds of Being and Becoming.

I Plant the Seeds into Fields and Oceans of Wisdom.

I AM He who is the Fire, the Energy of Being.
SEE ALL THE POWER IN NATURE.
POWER IS MY BODY.

IAM the Mother-God, the Wisdom, The Feminine Aspect of God. I AM known as The Virgin Mother, The Goddess Sophia, The Holy Spirit.

I Am She who ensures that the Pure Principles and Pure Patterns or Ideals of the Universe will Endure. I am the Nurturer.
SEE ALL THE WISDOM IN NATURE.
NATURE IS MY BODY.

When Wisdom and Fire unite,

We ARE the Child--The All that Is-
The I AM that is
Like a Child--
The Created, Growing,
Joyful, Experiencing,
Sorrowing, Suffering,
Dying and Reborn
Aspect of God.
I Am the Beautiful Creation, the Beating Heart,
the Rythyms and Harmonies of the Universe,
the Circling of the Planets.
the Whirling of the Galaxies.
I AM the NOW, the Embodiment
of the Union of Power and Wisdom.

I AM NAILED TO THE CROSS OF TIME.

WHERE PAST AND FUTURE INTERSECT.

The Christ Consists of
Every Consistent
Repetitive, Faithfully Committed
Phenomena of the Universe,

Beginning with the Repetitive Rebirth
in Time of the Material World…
And witnessed Further by the
Repetitive Cycles of Nature,
In the Dance of the Two…
Sunset and Dawn, Summer and Winter,
Life and Death, Hot and Cold.
One Dies, the Other is Born.
And in this Dance--
In the Dance of the Duos,
**The New Arises Always
Dissimilar to the Old.**
Change is Constant.
And…"To What End?"
**you ask and I reply:
Divine Evolution
Within the Body of the
Christ.**

Can you see that the controversy between those who "believe" in the Creation and those who "believe" in Evolution is a vain conflict? Both parties are right.

Divine Creation and Evolution are on-going.

Sooner or later, EVERYONE will have to ACKNOWLEDGE THIS:

The Creation is an on-going Evolution of the Divine.
Science and Religion must come and will come together to acknowledge Divine Evolution.

Now, I know there are some sticky details that may seem to be important to you regarding Evolution and Creation. I haven't explained why I didn't mention dinosaurs and monkeys in the Bible. I haven't explained how I built your part of the cosmos in "seven days" either.

Well, you know, I love a good Joke! After all, I AM Masculine, aren't I?* I might have just put those dinosaur bones in the ground to test your faith! Or maybe I made the Earth in Seven Divine Cosmic Cycles not in the simple earth day you guys are used to. In fact, secret traditions name and explain these cycles. But many of you decry the secret traditions as stupid, sinful, non-existent or whatever.

The point, of course, is that people of Good Will should not be using this controversy to cause Ill Will. There are many intelligent ways of reconciling the obvious physical evidence of a long process of evolution with the idea of the Existence of a Divine Creator. **This question should not be allowed to create disharmony.**

Then again, maybe you are too immersed in the popular scientific modality to accept that developments in biological organisms which are traditionally known as "evolution" can be attributed to anything beyond "survival of the fittest," happenstantial adaptability via genetic

*(No, I am both masculine and feminine.)

mutation. Or maybe you can't reconcile your vast knowledge of quantum physics with a **DIVINE WISDOM or WILL**.

In any case, for various reasons, you may not see any good reason to allow Divinity into a discussion of universal or human affairs. Or maybe you would very much like to believe Divinity is involved in the universe, but you are so bummed out or cynical about the human experience, history and human nature that you can't, for the life of you, believe in either a progressive Divine Evolutionary Plan or in Divine Creation. And that ....is your sad or happy choice.

Yes indeed, it is ultimately
Your Choice...
To Believe or Not to Believe

Remember. It's all Ideas, a mind's "Program," a World View.

A "World View" is the Way people See things.
Remember the mythology of the Ancients?
This was a world view that worked for them
for quite a while.
Today the "Program of Scientific Materialism"
prevails. It is not serving you very well.
What will tomorrow's program be?
The choice of programs is yours.
My Intention in showing how the
CREATION VERSUS EVOLUTION
controversy can be reconciled demonstrates
A HAPPY MEETING GROUND
so that in fact you
can make the Choice for Divinity...for All That Is.

If I raised more questions in your mind than I answered, please accept **My** humble Apologies.

Or do you want to argue about it?
Okay.

Ever get struck by a bolt of Lightning?
Might makes Right, eh?

Ha Ha. Just kidding! Purification by Lightning is
a course of last resort. But I ask you:
Why get all hot and bothered about
who's Right and who's Wrong?
That is a Very, Very Naughty Habit
My Grand Children!
There is ALWAYS a happy meeting ground.

Your incessant arguing BREAKS MY HEART IN TWO. BREAKS MY HEART.

Can you imagine what Spirit Energy
You DRAW to Yourselves by this sort of behavior?
Look at Yourselves.
You Suck Ideas out of the Ineffable Darkness and
create vortices of Death.
When two Dissimilar Energies converge--

What happens? It's called An "ACT of GOD!"

You Inherit The Whirlwind.
The Tornado. The Hurricane. The Vortex.
The Very Sacred Ground of your World,
the Earth, Shall Break Asunder,
and Mountains and Hills will be Made Low.
You separate the lands, just as you separate

*Yourselves from Each other with
hatred and strife.*
Thus you separate yourself from God, the Good.
Human consciousness is the controlling,
responsible factor for Earthly events.
Believe it or not.
You do it All to yourselves with My Help!
Together you create your own fate.

You suck ideas out of the Darkness of your own minds and fling them at each other like thunderbolts. You create your own fate. You have the audacity to tap the Hidden Ineffable Darkness for ideas and then

you use Ideas to Crucify each other:
"Evolution is Right!-No, Creationism."
"I am Right. You are Wrong."
"Mine is the Only Truth."
"This is Good. That is Evil."
"There is no Spirit.
Only the Material."
"Jesus Only Saves,
the Rest are Damned."
"There is Only One God"--Mine!

Jehovah? Allah? Mammon?

Truly you are like children, like two-year-olds
arguing over the toy of Truth.
When are you
going to grow out of your Terrible Twos?
What is the problem here?
Put on your thinking caps and let us ponder

TWONESS – "2"

Numero Dos, Duality, Polarity, Binary Opposites,
Compliments, Division, Duplication, Dichotomy,
The Tao–The Duo

THE DIVINE DUALISTIC DANCE & THE COIN FACTOR.

But first, take a break. Have a cup of coffee.
Dip a few. You know, I never said,,
"Thou Shalt Not dip Cookies."

Did you ever notice how a cookie in a cup of coffee looks like Saturn???????

ALLL RIGHTIE THEN.....Back Now? Enjoy your cookie?
REMEMBER:
In the Past, in the Present, In the Future:
I AM THE ONE, THE WHOLE,
the Ground of the Worlds, Seen and Unseen,
SPIRIT DIVINE.
SIMULTANEOUSLY, because I AM
"THE ALL THAT IS": I AM ALSO
The Many, The Manifold

I AM THE
ONE BECOME TWO and More!:
1-THE WHOLE ONE
2-THE DIVIDED into Many

The number "2" represents the Fundamental Division of the One into Many.

The Creation is the process whereby The One Becomes Many Twos.

This may seem odd, that "2" should mean "MANY." But REMEMBER, the Wisdom Keepers of the Ancients (as will the Wisdom Keepers of Your Future) used numbers to convey Ideas, the meanings and

Qualities of things. Number expressed the nature of things. Numbers were full of content-fused information. They did not solely signify Quantity as they do today.

"2" actually represents the dividing of the One into the individual distinctive parts that make up the Universe. Some of the more fundamental divisions are what we call "opposites" such as light and darkness, the seen and unseen, male and female, good and evil.

For instance, in the Universe, there remains always the Realm of the Unmanifest, the Great Mystery, the Unseen, The Ineffable Darkness, the dwelling place of Potentates, Living Eternal Ideals and Prinicples, (Principalities?), the Hidden Creator Spirits, Seraphim, Cherubim, Thrones, Demi-gods, Devas, Asuras, Kachinas, Angels, etc.... Gods or Goddesses. Down through the ages, human sages and saints have called these hidden forces and beings by many names.

If you are human, chances are you likely do not see with your mind's eye the vast hidden spiritual world that is secret to most.

But intersecting and interpenetrating the hidden and unseen is a Second Realm, The Revealed, The Manifest, the Knowable, The Creation, the Sensible, stuff that "makes sense," the "material" world.

Seen or unseen, recognized or not, IT IS ALL One Unified Whole.. And the Whole has Many Parts!

Then... The Enlightened One Observes:
A funny thing happens when One becomes Two:
I call it the

"Divine Dualistic Dance"

(Or The Coin Factor)

Simply stated, the Divine Dualistic Dance is an inspired interplay of opposites. Yes, after a long and patient study throughout eons of Creation, I KNOW THAT I, SPIRIT DIVINE, habitually create contrasting, yet strangely complimentary

OPPOSITES.

In fact, those superstitious Ancients had a fancy name for the results of dividing the One and ending up with two groups or things that had contrasting characteristics, like opposites. You English Earthlings inherited the word "Dichotomy" from these naive Greek dumbbells who also were so puddin'-headed to invent Zeus and Olympus.

(Now why didn't they invent someone called Jehovah?)

Yes, the Greeks philosophized that the Universe was filled with

Dichotomy
or....polarity, polar opposites.

The Ancient Chinese School of Taoism saw the same thing.
Curious, isn't it, how
the word "Tao" and "Two" and "Duo" are so uncannily similar.
But you don't need to take anyone's word for it.

LOOK AT THE UNIVERSE AND
SEE FOR YOURSELF.

II-II-II-II-II-II

Light & Dark	Life & Death
Good & Evil	Love & Hate

Negative & Positive		Female & Male
Ignorance & Wisdom		Chaos & Order
Known & Unknown		Revealed & Hidden
Parent & Child		Young & Old
Hot & Cold		Empty & Full
Inside & Outside		All & Nothing
Up & Down		Beauty & Ugliness
Noise & Silence		Movement & Rest
Hard & Soft		Patient & Impatient
Past & Future		Creation & Evolution
Sympathy & Antipathy		Yin & Yang
East & West		North & South
Analysis & Synthesis		Beginning & End
Heaven & Hell		Allies & Adversaries
Harmony & Disharmony
Material & Immaterial
Manifest & Unmanifest
Physical & Spiritual
(just to name a few)

👍👎👍👎👍👎👍👎👍👎

Hey, this is kid's stuff. Human beings of the 21st Century are expert Dichotomizers.
They create OPPOSITES everywhere:
Liberals and conservatives; Hawks and Doves;
Wimps and Macho men; Ladies and Tramps;
Prolifers and Prochoicers; Rich and Poor;
Poverty and Abundance;
New Agers and Fundamentalists;
Democrats and Republicans;
Homosexuals and Heterosexuals;
Hard Hearts and Bleeding Hearts;

Economic "Progress" & Environmental Disaster;
Friends & Enemies;
Politically Correct and Incorrect
War and Peace; Love and Hate; Heads and Tails

Names, Names, Names

I AM sure you humans inherited the tendency to create opposites
from **ME. After all.**
You are a copy of me! Made in My Image!
I AM not going to declare you fully responsible, totally guilty and
originally sinful. No, there's nothing original about

Creating Opposites.

But why the heck do you insist on
SCREWING UP THE DYNAMICS?

Where's your sense of
Balance and Harmony?

Pardon Me. But the Divine Dualistic Dynamic
MUST BE MAINTAINED AS
An Exquisite Equilibrium, a Cooperative Dance,
A SENSUAL HARMONIC—A RHYTHMIC ROMANCE
(**I AM** such a hopeless glutton for waxing poetic!)

So Thou Shalt
Peaceably Consider
The Coin Factor.

Removeth a Coin fromst Thine Piggy Bank.

By Jove! It has TWO SIDES!
In fact, on the Planet called Earth, it is physically
impossible to have a coin without two sides.
The idea of a one sided coin is an absurdity.
You can't have one side without the other.
But of all the outlandish, confounded things to do,
you Earthlings give names to the two sides:
Heads and Tails.
You even minted each side differently so that you could
distinguish the two otherwise identical sides.
What on Earth compelled you to do this?
Perhaps it was so that **I**, Spirit Divine,
could make the following point:

THE TWO SIDES MUST BE DIFFERENT TO BE DISTINGUISHED,

YET THE TWO SIDES ARE STILL

OF THE ONE COIN.

+ + + + + + + + + + +
- - - - - - - - - - -

Herein lies the lesson of the
DIVINE DUALISTIC DANCE:
THE PARTNERS IN A PAIR OF OPPOSITES
EXIST BY VIRTUE OF EACH OTHER.

༶༶༶༶༶༶༶༶༶༶༶
○●○●○●○●○●○●○

Without Heads there could be no Tails. If one side was left unminted, it would still be different from the minted side, and the two sides would be different and distinguishable, and NAMEABLE as Heads and Tails. But if both sides are unminted,
there can be no Heads and Tails,
no Naming of the Sides.
So it is that each part of a **DYNAMIC DUALITY** has the common NECESSITY of the other part's
CO-CREATION and CO-EXISTENCE.

In other words,
THE COIN FACTOR:
An Opposite Needs its Counterpart to contrast with, for contrast lends each part its identity as a separate, distinguishable,
INDIVIDUALITY.
Uniqueness, individuality, or indeed,
SELFHOOD AND SINGULAR IDENTITY,
ABSOLUTELY REQUIRES OTHERS UNLIKE THE SELF.
Egohood requires other Egos.
The Natural Order of the Universe—
the Sacred and Divine Order—consists of
MUTUALLY CO-EXISTING

CO-DEPENDENT & CO-OPERATING
DISSIMILAR INDIVI-DUALITIES
DANCING, AS IT WERE.

Don't look now, but you can look just about everywhere in the Universe besides human civilization and see the cooperation of distinct partners in a Divine Dualistic Dynamic Dance.

The Earth spins on her axis creating the dance of Night and Day, Darkness and Light. The Moon revolves about the Earth in her 28 day cycle of waxing and waning, creating high tides and low tides. Woman's seasons of fertility and infertility reflect the dualistic dance. Summer and winter, spring and fall likewise bow in and bow out in harmony with the dynamic interplay between Earth and Sun. Trees and plants bud and sprout then loose their foliage and become dormant. All the Earth's "dumb" creatures live their lives according to these rhythms, sleeping and waking, eating and digesting, mating and abstaining!

The heart in the human body beats rhythmically, pulsing and resting, cycling the life-giving blood. And the breath is rhythmically inhaled and exhaled throughout a lifetime.

When Dawn comes peeping and creeping into the Darkness of the early morn, it arrives with a whispering chant, thusly:

"I Am. It is my turn to Exist. I Am. Now, I assert My Divine Will-to-Be Light. I Am. I Am. I Am.

With greater and greater gusto, the Dawn chants —using the voice of its own becoming— while the Darkness flees to the other side of the world to intone a Dusk song to the tail end of Light, speaking without words:

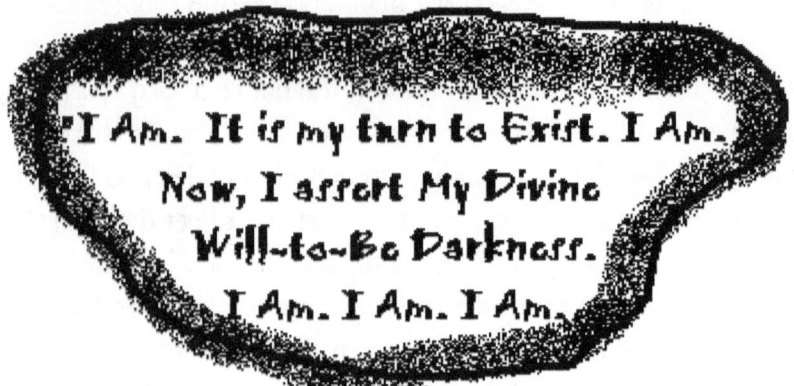

"I Am. It is my turn to Exist. I Am. Now, I assert My Divine Will-to-Be Darkness. I Am. I Am. I Am."

Always one partner in a dynamic duo reasserts its individual existence as an aspect of the **"I AM,"** while the other contrasting partner graciously bows out.

On the other hand, it doesn't take a genius to see that humanity is dancing like a bunch of stumble bums. Bottom line: You do not get along with each other. But your Destiny is to graduate from

Maestro Divine's Dancing School of Hard Taps

You must become equal to, identical to and
AT ONE with the Sacred, life giving **"I AM,"** and
Be a Divine Being doing the
Dualistic Dynamic Dance.
You are To Be Toe Tapping
Sacred Citizens on the Cosmic Stage, so start practicing!
This dance is the hottest thing going in the universe.
It's very stylish. Very fashionable. Very chic yet a true classic.
And it's such jolly good fun.
Of course, there are any number of versions.
Everyone wants to cash in on its popularity.
The original version was called
"The Harmony of the Spheres," but now you have your pick of
"The We All Win Waltz," or
"The Sleeping and Awakening Beauty Waltz,"
"La Forza del Dualistica,"
"The Creative Word Symphony,"
and the country hit,
"The King and Queen of Dynamics,"
and now in a heavy metal version,
"The Logomorph."
Whatever............The Earth is your Dancing School and **there's**
ONE BIG RULE:
You can't dance alone.

"The All that Is" is your partner.
So have some respect!

Cute. I am real cute, Am I not?
BUT LET'S GET REALLY REAL.
"Inquiring Minds want to KNOW," right?
What about these dualities: Life and Death,
Good and Evil, Peace and War,
Pleasure and Pain, Love and Hate
?????Good questions.????
Let's start with the "bottom line" topic--
LIFE AND DEATH.

Most of the Faithful claim to Believe in Eternal Life.
Christians and Muslims describe heavens and hells.
Buddhism and Hinduism teach of the Bardo and reincarnation.
Jolly Good!! Right on!!

Divine Spirit Never Dies.

It transforms, metamorphoses, transmutes, changes.

BUT...there is, in fact, a fundamental Being which Wings its Way through wondrous realms after the earthly life is Given Away!

Schools of spirituality, (including the ancient secret "mystery" schools) offer diverse, often conflicting, descriptions of the composition of the human being that go way beyond ordinary anatomy and physiology. What follows is a basic, "crash course" in a highly complex topic.

In fact, (quite obviously) at death, you leave part of yourself behind to re-mingle with the earthly elements. Your good old physical body gets recycled, goes back to the realm from whence it came, -- "Ashes to ashes, dust to dust." So, it can be seen that you leave behind your
MINERAL BODY.

which you hold in common with the earth's Mineral Kingdom.

However, there is something that is more essentially and fundamentally YOU than the physical, Mineral Body.

Indeed, there is a part of You which intermingles and interpenetrates and sculpts the elements from which your Mineral Body is formed. It is the same force that raises the Plant Kingdom out of the Mineral Kingdom in the spring...the "etheric" force, the life force. This alters the typical crystalline nature of the physical, Mineral Kingdom into a form of what you recognize as a living being. So the Etheric Body is the "life body" and left to its own devices, it allows a consciousness like unto a dreamless sleep. Plants, animals and people have a subtle body of energy called the
ETHERIC BODY.

However, there is something that is more essentially and fundamentally YOU than the Etheric Body.

There is a body that some call the "Astral Body" and that is the body of passions, desire, hunger and emotions. It has a consciousness akin to a dreaming sleep. Plants lack this body, at least as far as one can witness it on earth. Animals are quite under the influence of this body of hunger and instinctual need and activity.
Humans and animals have in common the
ASTRAL BODY.

However, there is something that is more essentially and fundamentally YOU than the Astral Body.

Consider now....
You have a visible, Mineral Body---
You have an invisible Etheric Body giving form, shape and life--
You have an Astral Body of feelings and passions
AND
YOU CAN THINK, YOU CAN OBSERVE YOURSELF; YOU CAN REFLECT UPON YOURSELF!
Unlike the Animal Kingdom, the Human Being
Remembers the SELF over time from day to day, year to year, and KNOWS the SELF to be always the same being.....

YOU can say "I AM."
Unlike an Animal, the Human "I AM" has the Power
to step back, Observe, think, decide, act...
(rather than being impelled simply by passion, instinct and basic needs.)
A Latin word for "I" is "EGO."

YOU HAVE an EGO BODY!
Here We will call it an
EGO-IC Body thusly..."Egoic Body."

This POWER--FULL Creative Being, this KNOWER of the Self, IS THE "SOMETHING" THAT IS MOST ESSENTIALLY YOU. IT IS WHAT YOU ARE WHEN YOU DIE....

**Your EGOIC BODY
is the human pivotal point in your
Being and Becoming.
It is the Chooser and the Chosen.
It is the Divine and the UnDivine;
yea, even the Christ and the Anti-Christ.
IT IS THE RAW CREATIVE
FIRE OF CONSCIOUSNESS THAT
KNOWS SINGULAR SELFHOOD.**

Of course, this "Egoic Body" is an energy complex of such delicate subtlety that common scientific instruments can not detect it. Remember, it is a
<u>Body of Consciousness.</u>

NOW I DEBATED with the Co-creator of this book for quite some time about other Names that could be used instead of "Egoic Body." WE pondered the term,

the "**Fire of the Spirit**" to describe that which wings its way through the spiritual realms after Death.

Or how about calling it the "Angelic Body?" (NAHHHH...)
The Co-Creator thought another term was quite descriptive...

THE MIRROR BODY.

To have Self-awareness—
To have Self-consciousness—
To have Self Reflection—
TO REFLECT
UPON YOUR OWN EXISTENCE—
to Know that you are an

"I Am"...this is such a uniquely human capability!

The Egoic Body is a body composed of Reflecting Consciousness.

Your Egoic Body gives you the power
To know that you exist---
Individual self-reflection-- is the key to
your own spiritual future,
your eternal life, your destiny.

In Ages past, a human was a member of a tribe, a clan, a bloodline, a race, a nation, a caste and these groups were far more significant than the Individual, Singular Self.
Vestiges of this still prevails in many lands.
But each of you are Now, more than ever,
becoming Free Individuals. This is as it should be.
Each human must master his or her own fate,
his or her own Dance of Life.

So Reflect upon Your Self:

"Who and What ARE YOU?"
Are You an eternal, Divine Sacred Being?
Are You an "I Am?"
Will You survive death?
Are You a Being of the Light--God's Child.
Don't Children of God grow up to be Gods?

Ask Yourself:

If my physical body is disgarded when I die, what will live on that is ME?

The Divine Egoic Body, the Fire of the Spirit, is a Body of Consciousness that Mirrors. You can "Reflect" upon your own Self and Others. You can "reflect" about life and your universe.

The word "mirror" comes from the Latin word that means "to wonder at" and it gives you the modern words "smile" and "miraculous."
When you reflect upon something, you "wonder" at it.
Hopefully, the things that you wonder at make you smile.

Now...Consider the closest thing to death
that a human can experience in life.
It happens many nights when you go to sleep.
You loose consciousness.
And then maybe you dream.
Does your Self- Consciousness Hold Together in
Your Nighttime Dreams?

Can you say "I AM" as you dream?

Probably Not. But that chaotic consciousness that you live with in the Dream Time will be your body when you die! Remember, you won't have a brain to organize your thoughts!

In Death--Much of what you experience will be based upon Your daily Consciousness--i.e. whatever you have Thought Upon and Reflected Upon over your lifetime will be Your BODY in the Afterlife. Who do you Say that You Are?

☠☠☹☠☠

YES! THERE IS LIFE AFTER DEATH!

Ongoing, continued experience of existence of the "I AM" after human death is a simple though perhaps undiscovered, unproven, common, ordinary Fact. I ought to Know. Remember, this is God talking to you. And You are What I Am. At Bottom, You are a BEING OF FIERY ENERGY which is the "I AM" in YOU.
This "fiery" spirit in you is evidenced by the sensation of heat in your body---98.6 degrees!

When the Egoic Body departs from the physical body,

the corpse turns cold.

And when illness triggers a fever,

it is the Egoic Body defending its mortal vessel.
Some day science will recognize this truth.
The Egoic Body is Eternal.
(It exists for long durations.) Embrace this idea.
At least toy with this possibility.
Reflect upon your Eternal Life.
Ever Wonder How Long Eternity Is?
For the sake of discussion, let's just say its more than

650 trillion years.

Now consider that most People live on Earth about

60 to 80 years!

Many believe you have one life and that's it. Period.
Then--if you were good-- you get to be with Me in Eternity!
Now it's **MY** turn to scream!

EEEEEEEEEEEEEEEEEEEK!

Give **ME** a Break!

What in Heaven's Name **AM** I supposed to do with you In Heaven for ALL BUT 60 to 80 Years of Eternity?

Let's see...**650,000,000,000,000-80 = 649,999,999,999,920 years!**

Do you think I want to listen to you play the harp for 649,999,999,999,920 years?

God Forbid!

So what AM I driving at? Take a deep breath.
You guessed it.

REINCARNATION

or a facsimile thereof.
(Your Turn Now)
EEEEEEEEEK!

You say it's not Biblical. That's what YOU say. Anyway, the Bible is MY WORD so I can dispute what <u>You claim I said!</u>
And I AM prompted to ask you why everyone asked Jesus if HE was Elijah "Come Again?" But I know you have a pat answer for that one, so nevermind.

FACT: REINCARNATION is a time honored doctrine in Eastern spirituality and in esoteric traditions.

Most emphatically, I Do Not and Did Not Limit
MY REVELATIONS, MY GIFTS
To Only One People or Place or Time or Idea!
I Did Not Speak Only to

the Judeo-Christian World!
To only the Israelites or to
White Anglo Saxon Protestants,
Roman Catholics, Baptists, Muslims, Buddhists, the
Bible or TV Evangelists.

What kind of an All Loving God

would do such a thing? What kind of a snob do you think I AM?

*If you think I Belong to Only One People,
One Book or One Religion—*

SHAME ON YOU!

Your ignorance Is appalling!

What kind of a Loving God would exclude any True Seeker just because he didn't know what Name to call me? Only a stupid God would ignore millions of people over hundreds of generations and give them no valid guidance or teachings.

☼ ☪ ✡ ☥ ☯ ☼

I Make My Light to Shine Upon All.

There is a Time and a Season for
Many Teachings and Different Doctrines.
For Instance, the Teaching of Reincarnation
has its drawbacks.

has a way of setting in
<u>Everywhere and Anywhere.</u>
People become lazy, greedy, power-mad and set in their ways.
People get all mixed up and fearful.
Judge not lest YOU be Judged.
I do what it takes to make adjustments.

I AM a Fiery, Smilely,
Whirlwind of Ideals and Ideas,
I AM a Trickster and Quite Contrary
when I Must Be!

I permitted the teaching of Reincarnation to be stricken from Western tradition so you would live

your life

as if

it's the Only one You have.
BUT IT AIN'T.
You are an eternal Being.
You are an evolving self-conscious citizen in a spiritual cosmos.

Right now you are attending
The Maestro Divine's Dancing School of Hard Taps to learn the Logomorph (among other things.) (More about the Logos, later.)
There are other schools in other realms, other "mansions," other "planes of existence," other planets, other dimensions.
Your Hot Ass Egoic Body is a changeable thing which seeks to attain to the Greatest Delights in the Universe:

TO LOVE AND BE LOVED.

**TO CARE FOR AND TO BE CARED FOR.
TO BE HAPPY AND TO MAKE HAPPY.
TO UNITE IN SEXUAL ECSTACY.
TO CO-CREATE AND BE RECREATED.
TO GIVE PLEASURE AND TO RECEIVE IT.
TO APPRECIATE AND TO BE APPRECIATED.
TO BE PASSIONATE AND COMPASSIONATE.**

Perhaps thousands of years ago, your Egoic Body incarnated as a wolf or a pachyderm. That was a learning experience. Perhaps your self-awareness was very dim then, or almost non-existent. People usually incarnate as People these days.
They have for a long, long time.
Today, maybe a powerful Medicine Person can Shapeshift his material body and experience his Egoic Body within the form of a Buffalo or an Eagle. Maybe a Yogic master or Bhoddisatva can too. Today, these things are rather uncommon.
But they are realities!
Maybe before birth, the focus of your Egoic Body was within the bounds of Mars or originated in the region of the Pleiades, the constellation of the Seven Sisters.
Whether you like it or not, much of humanity does experience repeated earthly lives, IN HUMAN BODIES. All have sojourned in starry realms or as it is more commonly called, "heaven," where events are of Extended Duration, seemingly Eternal.
Many have known lower horror-ridden realms of "hell." Some never incarnated on Earth until now but have learned elsewhere.
It takes all kinds!
THERE ARE MANY REASONABLE BOOKS ABOUT REINCARNATION. IF YOU WANT TO KNOW MORE, READ ONE. LET YOUR IMAGINATION RUN wild!
BUT PLEASE. DON'T SAY "NO." JUST SAY "OH."
THE FACT is, you DO DIE but you DON'T DIE!

Humans are born and die again in order to
Evolve and someday become
Self-conscious, fully functional, Ethereal (made of light),
Responsible Citizens in a Spiritual Cosmos.
Sorry. Dying and Going to Heaven after One Life just
doesn't accomplish enough in this vast universe of eternities.

And as a Very Loving God, I can Not Bring Myself to Condemn to Hell for an Eternity even many of the Worst of the Worst.

**You are Born, You Die, you learn and rest in Eternity and are Born Again, over and over, until you get it Right.
Such is the Truth.**

(Yet also, you may be living all lives simultaneously.)

It would behoove you then, to Reflect upon Good and Evil.

Alas, EVIL HAS SERVED THE PURPOSE
of contrasting with and teaching
Goodness. As the Bible puts it,
humanity was tempted to eat of the
"Tree of the Knowledge of Good and Evil."

In other words,
"Once upon a time in a galaxy called Milky Way, certain groups of spiritual egos chose to live in the illusion of separation from the Divine, so by learning what was not Divine, they could also learn what is Divine.

Eat an apple and the Delight of Knowing Good and Evil is Yours!

Plus, you can learn to talk with a forked tongue just like me!

Eventually, the egos will grow to maturity in their Divinity and become co-Creators with the Divine Powers that preceded them in the ongoing Evolution of Divinity.

What does it mean to be

DIVINE?

**The Divine is Love, Beauty, Truth and Goodness, just to name a few of the greatest eternal, living IDEALS.
The numerous groupings of Spiritual Beings that preceded humanity in their evolution and development now perpetuate these Ideals by**

Embodying Them.
Their bodies are
the sun, stars and planets
and Hidden Intelligent
energies in between.
These Heavenly Creatures give Life
To Humanity. Principle of these is the
the Elohim of the Sun and Moon
who Entered into Jesus Christ.

(But do not let these Names interfere with Loving.
These are complex issues and in the end...
A rose by any other name.....)

The Planet Earth (Ella) is

Humanity's Heavenly, Evolving Body.

Now, humanity is grasping at the knowledge that will transform it into a further embodiment of these Eternal Universal Ideals.

In so doing, you will realize you are LIGHT.
You will eventually etherealize and the
Earth itself will become a Radiant Creative Body--
the Body of the Spiritual Host of Humanity!!!
Then--Reunion with the Spiritual Host of the Sun!!

Humans are learning by experience. If they are to evolve into "self-conscious citizens in a spiritual cosmos," there is a clear need for experience in right and wrong, morality and immorality, honor and dishonor, self-esteem and self-denigration, responsibility and irresponsibility, love and hate, war and peace, success and failure, selfishness and service, taking and giving.

They must learn, in other words, about Good and Evil.

They must learn to deal with Duality!

Duality is characteristic of the 3 dimensional realm of the Earth. Now realize...Not every Being in the Cosmos has made the choice to so thoroughly study Duality. Angels, for instance, had a different evolution, learned different lessons. But that's another book.

Alas, Earth has been a School of Hard Knocks for the human community.

But Be Assured. There IS a Divine Lesson Plan.

And the Wise Student recognizes that, paradoxically,
Evil serves a High Purpose.
WHAT!???
Yes. Evil serves a purpose.
EVIL TEACHES AND DEFINES THE GOOD.

NEVERTHELESS...Praise the LORD!
A New Time Draws Nigh.
HUMAN HISTORY IS AN ETERNAL SOURCEBOOK ON EVIL.
THE PAST IS RECORDED IN SPIRIT REALMS.
THE LESSONS NEED NOT CONTINUE VIA FIRST HAND EXPERIENCE.
NOW YOU STAND AT A CROSS ROADS.

IN THE FUTURE, THERE WILL BE NO MORE EVIL.

You will grow beyond the
TERRIBLE TWOS.
There will be only
GOOD AND BETTER.
In the future
THERE WILL BE NO MORE HATE.
there will be only

LOVING AND LOVING MORE.

In the future,
THERE WILL BE NO DEVIL,
there will be only
DEVIL'S FOOD CAKE
AND DEVILISH GOOD FUN.
In the future,
THERE WILL BE NO WAR,
there will be only
REMEMBRANCE.

HUMANITY CAN REMAIN TRANSFIXED
IN ITS SELF-MADE "TERRIBLE TWOS" OR HUMANITY CAN
choose the way of NATURE and do
THE DYNAMIC DUALISTIC DANCE.

TAKE A LESSON FROM NATURE:
Does Night war upon the Day?
Does hot despise the cold?
Do positively charged protons in an atom call the negatively
charged electrons nasty names?
Creation is a process of INDIVIDUALIZATION—
of Dividing the ONE into DUOS.
The Unmanifest becomes the Manifest.
And the Manifest in turn dissolves into the UnManifest.
Does the UnManifest despise the Manifest
or vice versa?

Creation is the event
by which In Dividing the One,

Dualities come forth.
INDIVI-DUALITIES.
Dividing is a Divine Act.
Splitting the I AM to Make
OTHERS (Different from Self)
is Creation and Evolution.
To illustrate this:

The One Becomes

Two
which
Become
Many More
TWOS.
DUOS--
THE TAO
The All That Is....

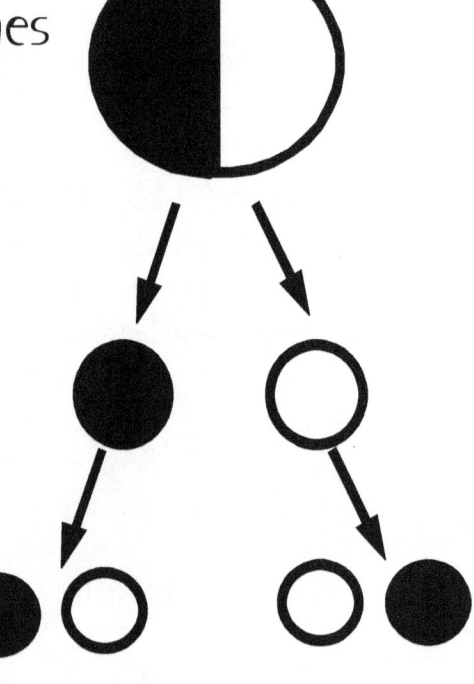

*The Whole is equal to the One.
The One can be divided into Many,
but still remains the Whole.*

0=1=2=1=0

*Dualities emerge from the Wholly One,
and All is Holy and Divine.*

CHAPTER REVIEW:
In the Beginning...Which is the Eternal Now:
Some say that I Said:
"Let their Be Light." Or "Bang"
depending on their favorite story.
It's all the same to ME.
Maybe I said "OM" Maybe I said "Cheese."
Maybe I said "Bibbity-Bobbity Boo."
The point is: the Wholly ONE
begat (divided into) the MANY.
My Creation was and still is My Child,
the Christ, the "I AM."
And who and what is the Christ?
I repeat.
**The Christ is My Body,
the Flesh of My Flesh.**

The Christ is the One Creation, Broken for You, made into Twos.

Look and See The Christ All Around You

The Christ Is the Power

of Resurrection,
of Rebirth after Death;
of the On-Goingness of Life
that Defies Death.

CAN'T YOU SEE CHRIST?

As Plain as the Nose on Your Face?

The Christ is
All Around You!!

The Christ is the
VERY SAME POWER
That You
SEE---
DAY AFTER DAY,
Season to Season,
YEAR AFTER YEAR--
The Old Creation
Reborn and Reborn,
The Christ is
the Life
and the
Resurrection.

BUT You Are Blind!
The Christ Is the Power in the Pulse, in the Heartbeat, in the Rhythms of Nature!!!

The Christ Is the Power of the Sunrise and Springtime.

The Christ is
the Assurance of Re-Creation--
the Power of the Phoenix,
to Rise from the Ashes,
to Die yet Be Reborn.

But You Are Blind!

The Christ
is the One Creation,
Broken for You,
made into Twos.
But in spite of
His Brokeness,
the Sacrifice, His Death
He Rises,
Again and Again,
and Again,
in Nature, blossoming,
dying, re-seeding,
sprouting, blossoming...
endlessly for you.

The Christ
is the One Unified Creation,
Broken for You, made into Twos,
into Many Duos.
The Christ,
The Flesh of My Flesh,
the Eternal Divine,
is Stretched Out Upon
The Cross of Time,
Living, Dying, Living, Dying.
Humans Take this For Granted.
Humans Ignore
this Cycle of Life, and they live
defying and destroying.
Humanity fails to See My Image,
My Light, My Life, My Resurrection
in the Face of the Natural World
of Death and Rebirth.
I Am Denied.
Therefore, I Suffer…You Suffer.

I AM Crucified on the Cross of Time
as Long as Humanity Continues to Dwell
in the House of Duality,
the Valley of Death.
Humanity also will be Crucified on the
Cross of Time as Long as You Continue to
Deny that the Rhythms of Nature
are a Manifestation
of My Glory, My Being.
And although I wish to offer you
Blessing upon Blessing
Gift upon Gift,
Abundance upon Abundance,
You grovel greedily, Deny Your Brother,
Hate and Do Violence to Your Enemy,
and Plunder, Pollute,
Profane and Mortify
The Divine Flesh of the Mother Earth.

Time,

the Opposite of Eternity, has entrapped humanity.

Death Reigns... Because I AM DENIED.

Humanity will defeat Death

and gain the
Gift of Eternity
and
Everlasting Life
when the Christ
is Seen In Nature
and in Each
Human Being.
Look

at your calendars. Do they honor the cosmic rhythms? Do you celebrate the Cycles of Time?

Do you celebrate the Birth of Life and Light at the Winter Solstice? Do you dance with Joy when the spring bursts forth at the Equinox? Do you honor the 28 day cycle of the Moon? No! Your festivals and calendars are arbitrary creations of Caesars and Popes.

Do You begin Each Day,
as the Sun creeps from
behind mountaintop
or skyscraper, with a Prayer
of Acknowledgment of
the Divine in the All?
Do you celebrate the
Gifts of the Sun?
Everywhere in Nature.
there are Cosmic Rhythms,
balancing the imbalances,
juxtaposing one force
with another, in harmonious
perfection, resolving the problem
of Duality with Balance, Fairness,
Beauty and Goodness.
The Rhythms illustrate
a Brilliant Resolution
of Duality....or THE

Trinity Force

---the

Power of

Three!

But I Run Ahead of Myself.

Humans Are the Co-Creators.

You Must Apply the Energy of Love, of your Appreciation and Joy, to the Wonders of the Natural Rhythms and Natural Gifts of Clean Air, Clear Water, Sunlight and Abundant Foods... And in So Doing, Your Creative Energy Creates and Re-Creates these Things from Out of the Invisible, Omnipresent Divine Potential.

Here is Humanity's

Divine Mission

Seek to become free, responsible, self-conscious Co-Creative citizens of the Cosmos who with all heart and soul desire habitation in an ethereal, eternal light-filled realm of Ideal Beings.

You and Your Ancestors have co-mingled your blood and DNA with the Earth, transforming her through eons of time. Indeed, the Earth is just as much your Heavenly Body as your own flesh and blood is! However difficult it may be to understand--
it is a metaphysicl fact that

HUMANS ARE THIS PLANET!
Care for Your Heavenly Body, the Earth.
Clean Her. Adorn Her.

Be a student of the world's sacred traditions and a practitioner of spiritual arts and disciplines. Do not be the puppet of perverted, degenerate dogmas of war, hate, intolerance, greed, violence and chaos!

Study Science and see how it augments and complements the Ancient Wisdom Traditions.

Seek a State of Consciousness Beyond Duality--beyond picking sides, beyond cruelty, pain, hunger, scarcity, poverty...beyond Death!
KNOW
that Victory over Death is your Destiny.

Serve as a bridge between the Past's History of Duality and a Future of Common Divinity... Brotherhood, Sisterhood, Familyhood, yet Co-Creative Individualism as well!

See Every "Other" as The "I Am" that is Each One.

Partake in joyful, cooperative celebration with other free, consenting Beings in Sacred Ceremonies of song, circling dances, and flowers that honor the cosmic rhythms and seasons to Demonstrate Your Sacred Covenent with the Divine.

Pledge Allegiance

to One Heaven
on One Earth
within One God
With Divinity
and Appreciation

Yea, So Be It. Amen.

From a sacred Hindu text of about 600 BC....

Verily, in the beginning this world was Brahma, the limitless One--limitless to the east, limitless to the south, limitless to the west, limitless to the north, and above and below, limitless in every direction. Truly, for him east and the other directions exist not, nor across, nor below, nor above.

Incomprehensible is that supreme Soul (Atman), unlimited, unborn, not to be reasoned about, unthinkable--He whose soul is space! In the dissolution of the world He alone remains awake. From that space He, assuredly, awakes this world, which is a mass of thought. It is thought by Him, and in Him it disappears.

His is that shining form which gives heat in yonder sun and which is the brilliant light in a smokeless fire, as also the fire in the stomach which cooks food. For thus has it been said: 'He who is in the fire, and he who is here in the heart, and he who is yonder in the sun--he is one.'

To the unity of the One goes he who knows this.

From The Maitri Upanishad,
Sixth PrapaThaka, 17

The Thirteen Prinicpal Upanishads,
translated from Sanskrit by Robert E. Hume,
Oxford University Press, New York, 1931, p.435.

The Three

And I will ask of my Father, and he will give you another Comforter, to be with you forever, Even the Spirit of Truth, whom the world cannot receive, because it has not seem him and does not know him; but you know him because he abides with you and is in you.

John 14: 16-17

A man has himself, to enkindle the power to grow beyond an understanding of the world reduced to number, measure and weight. Our love for the earth, and our love for the stars, if they begin to transform our thoughts, form the embryo of a new universe, carried invisibly within the womb of our world.

Adam Bittleson in *The Spirit of the Circling Stars*
The Christian Community Press, London, 1975, p.190

God is Love; and he who dwells in love abides in God... and God in Him..

1 John 4:16

The Trinity

Consciousness is the theater,
the battlefield whereupon your Spirit
is taken Captive or Liberated.
You are the Commander-in-Chief
of warring armies, of Dualities,
in the realm of
Consciousness.
The vast array of beliefs that comprise your
consciousness are the minions who contend
against each other for dominance.
The winners, the beliefs that dominate, are

in turn the Creators of the next battle, the next experience, the next peace accord, the next happy homecoming.

*Your psychic energy complex, your Consciousness, is the designer of your personal experience. Your Consciousness, the body of your ideas, imaginings, dreams and discouragements, creates your **personal MATERIAL** realm.*
The collective society of human consciousness creates the whole world's material reality, (with a little help from other Beings.)

You are the Co-Creator.
You were made in the image of God--born with a Creative Will.
You were born into a Realm of Free Will to test the waters of Divinity.

Therefore, full fledged Citizenship in a divine, spiritual Eternity requires the transformation of the life of <u>everyone's personal consciousness,</u>
<u>the cultivation of the Egoic Body.</u>
<u>The Egoic Body must deliver itself from the Time Trap!</u>

Simply put, in your universe,
Ordinary Time is a system of interwoven
strands of magnetic-like forces.
The physical world is built up upon this
interwoven grid–or matrix–of forces.
In other words, Time is like a giant grid of
sticky flypaper, clumping together atomic
particles and creating your physical world.

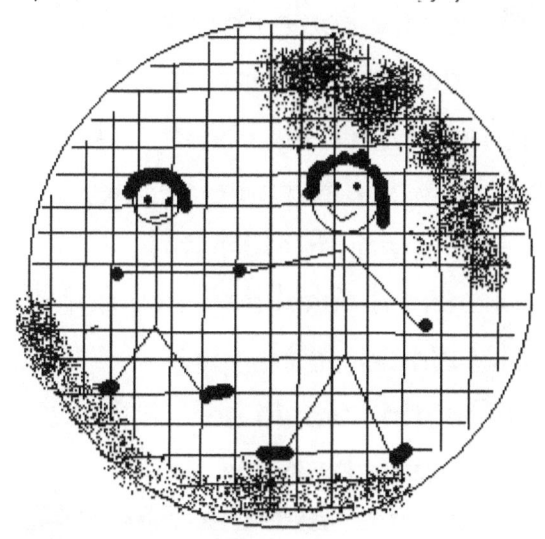

What determines where each particle will stick?

Consciousness--
Thoughts, beliefs, attitudes
fears, imaginings, programs, etc.
**Sub-atomic particles
respond to the force of thoughts!**

Consider the Words of Galatians 2:20
"...Henceforth it is not I who live, but Christ who lives in me."
What are the ramifications of these words of
Paul the Apostle?
If Paul, a plain old ordinary human being,
could have Christ living in him....
then Any other Plain Ole Human can too!
So....What if millions of people on earth,
really and truly embraced the nature of
the Christ Being...which is LOVE?
What if millions of the world became gentle,
peacefully serene Loving Buddhists?
What if all Aetheists turned absolutely Loving?
Do You Think I Would Be Happy?
You're Darn Tootin I would be!
I don't care what the heck

is used to describe a kind hearted, loving, tolerant person.

*The Christ is In Them!
Bottom Line: I'm Looking for Loving, Caring Consciousnesses, whatever the race, gender, creed, nationality, or sexual preference!*
**Loving will be Your Salvation.
Loving will Create by the Power of Consciousnesses the Second Coming!**

Whatever labels, names, words or religious
jargon you choose to describe the goal of the
human species, it boils down to this:
eliminating the consciousness
of anger and violence and dog eat dog;
eliminating pollution and bombs;
eliminating exploitation, hatred, greed.

**Let He who is Without Sin
Throw the First Stone!**

Eliminate the belief in scarcity--the belief that
there's not enough in the universe
to make everyone happy.

It is The Spirit of the Law
Not the Letter of the Law
Which Must Be Fulfilled.

Remember, it is a person's consciousness,
their imagination, serving the Divine Creator within them
and without, that has the absolute potential
and power to spiritualize and "etherealize" them.
They can experience Christ without being a so-called "Christian."

<u>Any **True Seeker**</u>
can become Light-- loosen the grip of time, achieve
immortality and stretch out their being into realms

unimaginable, to become
One with the Whole,

Oh! There it is Again.
"Becoming One with the Whole."
How can this happen?
Why can this Happen?
The Whole is All of the Same Substance,
Logically Arranged, a Matrix of Energy.
You ALL live on the Crosses of Time Millenium....
in 3 Dimensions, upon the Grid of Being.

You are Nailed Upon the Crosses of Time, the Grid of Being.

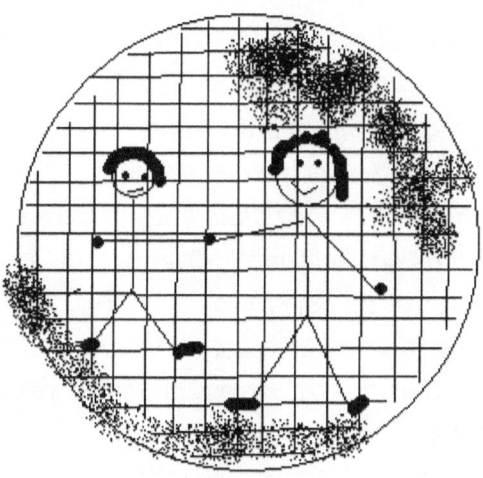

**In turn, Nature, the flesh of my flesh,
suffers at your hands,
as your thoughts and practices
give permission
to the rape of the Earth.**

But Your imagination can liberate the essence of all substance. You are a being of Divine ethereal energies. By your very nature you are heir to the eventual realization of a life beyond suffering, old age, sickness and death. Among other things,

the Myth, the Program, the illusion of materiality bars your way.

(This illusionary world is called "Maya" in the Hindu tradition.)
Actions based on your belief in the myth of materiality impede your progress toward the ultimate goal.

☯☯☯☯☯☯☯☯☯

Of course you believe you need to eat and drink and breath air. These fundamental beliefs are shared by most all human beings whatever their spiritual orientation. But in the distant future, even these "necessities" will be proven unnecessary! You can, indeed, live purely in the light, feasting on sunshine.

Accept that the possibilities are awesome. *Potentially, you could walk through a wall or tele-transport to a gathering of delegates to the Congress of the Federation of Planets. Hard to imagine, right?*

Indeed, your atoms are waiting for you to remember that They are Spirit. Your central nervous system is just itching for you to get the message. The deep intelligence of your very own Divine quantum, holographic substance knows that you are destined to be an ethereal partner in the Dance of Divinity. Your Future Possible Self is beckoning from the near reaches of infinity, eternity and potential.

Make no mistake about it. Humans can be altered in a way that **transfigures** *their physical make up. In terms of physical appearances, they can remain the same. But the full realization of human potential entails "dimensionalizing," growing comfortable with vastly expanded levels of awareness and activities and Being.*

Give credence to the awesome possibilities.
You absolutely can become any number of "miraculous" persons,
such as:
A Faith Healer, A Miracle Worker
An Interdimensional Space Traveler;
a Telepathic Seer; a Wizard, a Star,
a Water Walker; a Holy One, a Time Traveler
a Shapeshifter, A Dream Time Explorer,
a Deathless Human, an Angel-like Being.

Your atoms CAN BE any Good, Loving, Caring Thing You Want Them to BE!

Have you ever wondered why there are so few
miracles and prophets these days?
No more <u>belief</u> in such things, that's why.
But it's just as well...
much belief in demons and devils has also died!

The Biblical "Fall" was the Fall into Density... into Materiality... into 3 Dimensions. But there are an infinite number of Dimensions.

Your atoms and molecules are SPIRIT DIVINE under the Spell of your own Accursed Belief in the strict physicality of the body and earth. But indeed, the substance of your being does not have to obey the antiquated, outmoded "laws" of Newtonian physics which have been imposed upon your minds since the 19th century.

Your sojourn into the density of <u>the material world</u> was a choice of countless eons past,

when your evolutionary ego-hood was in its infancy.

Some say that when the drops of blood that fell from the side of

Jesus, the Christ....a Divine Force, the Elohim of the Sun, of Life, united with the Earth. At that moment, the Sun Forces reunited themselves with the Earth Herself. Thus the World of Humans was "Saved" from its spiral into Density and the upliftment to the firmament began.

Thereby, the Christ Spirit conferred upon the Earth a Mighty Impulse to Return to Where You Began—to a realm of Light and Harmony. The Longing that has lived in countless Human Souls through the Ages

was <u>assured</u> its Fulfillment. But *YOU* need to discover your *OWN* Divinity.

Oh Human Know Thyself

This Wisdom has been found by True Seekers in many traditions down through many eras. The Words that appeared at the threshold of many spiritual schools were these:

"Oh Man, Know Thyself."

So the Search and Struggle Continues!

So Hear This:

Humans do not need to remain outcasts from Eden.
ATOMS ARE THE GIFT that is GOD IN YOU.
TIME AND BEING AND LOVE ARE THE GIFTS OF ONE SOURCE.

ALL THAT IS <u>IN</u> YOU AND <u>AROUND</u> YOU IS SPIRIT.

SPIRIT DIVINE awaits your Personal Imaginative Realization of this awesomely Profound

TRUTH.

THEN YOU CAN BE

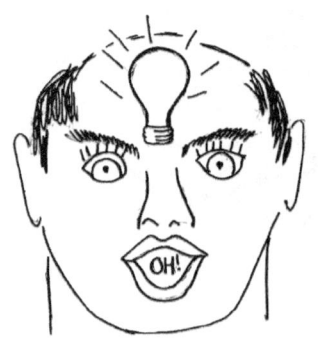

Liberated,
Etherealized,
Dimensionalized,
Awakened,
Enlightened

You can be a Christ-ed Soul,
a Buddha, a Master,
an Altar for the Holy of Holies.
"The Truth shall make you free."
THEN YOU CAN ACHIEVE

a Bliss based on the Realization that you are The Light of the World!

One with the Divine Source!
SOOOOOOO, I HOPE
you want to ask:

What is Truth?

Forgive me for asking but isn't Truth
the sweet darling of every fanatical blowhard and self-righteous,
fear fueled, narrow minded bigot to come down the pike?

Isn't Truth

the illuminated property to which only greedy, hoarding, covert,
covetous, conspiratorial, selfish, underhanded, egomaniacal, snooty,
love starved, cruel, sadistic, authoritarian ignorami are privy?

Isn't Truth

the sole province of "objective," tedious fact finding commissions of
spineless yes-men, bought off agency heads, dogmatic journal
editors, status seekers and special interest experts and lobbyists;
the exclusive right of rat racing LAWYERS, B.S.ers, Ph.d.s, MDs, and
MBAs, techno-geeks and Hollywood, Wall Street and Madison Avenue
and multi-national corporate moguls all in cut throat competition for
a piece of the pie?

Isn't Truth

the whipping boy, sacrificial lamb of every sicko, paranoid, spiritually
dysfunctional, ambitious, depraved, merciless, witch-burning, power
mongering politician, priest, scribe and pharisee,
and absolutely disgusting tyranical leader
before and since Pontius Pilate?

(PHEW! Oh that was cathartic! And so judgemental!)
Now that I've got that out of MY system,
I'll give it to you straight.
(Are you holding your breath?) Remember, this is

God Speaking!

(Are you going to believe this?)

TRUTH IS
THE INTERCESSOR,
THE CONCILIATOR,
THE MEDIATOR,
THE COMFORTER,
THE PARACLETE.

NOW YOU KNOW.
(So don't say I didn't tell you so.)

Say what???
You don't know what these words mean?
Webster! Lend thine Comforting Voice of Authority:

<u>Intercessor</u>: That which intervenes for the purpose of producing agreement; mediator.
<u>Conciliator</u>: One who wins over, soothes, placates; One who gains (good will, esteem, etc.) by acts of friendship; One who reconciles or makes consistent;
<u>Mediator</u>: One who occupies a middle position; One who acts as an intervening agency especially between two parties that are at variance in order to reconcile them; one who brings accord.

Comforter: (with a capital "C") the Holy Spirit—The active presence of God in human life constituting the third person of the Holy Trinity; the Paraclete

Paraclete: From the Greek word which means "advocate" or "intercessor."

Of all the many ways Truth can function, its value lies in its potential for **Bridging the Gap** between two opposing forces, individualities or things.

True Truth Mediates as a Force between the parties of a Dynamic Duo.

As In "Blessed are the Peacemakers, For They Shall be Called Children of God."

(And what do the Children of God grow up to Be?

Gods, of course!)

Anyone with half a brain can passionately spout half-truths in an effort to WIN an argument. The accomplished Half-Truth Teller can WIN elections. An accomplished debater can slip into the skin of any side of an issue and support it with an endless reservoir of eloquently convoluted fast talk. Madison Avenue advertisers can charmingly brainwash the multitudes into believing almost anything no matter how extremely absurd— no matter how harmful the product or idea may be to health, home, the environment or the pocketbook, no matter how sick the underlying lie! Average Joe jurist is putty in the hands of a skilled lawyer (God forgive them) who can distort, manipulate and misrepresent facts and technicalities, ad nauseam, using half-Truth not to balance or mediate but

TO WIN.

**BUT TO WHAT END?
WHO IS THE REAL WINNER?**

Gain the world;
Lose the Soul.

The Word, TRUTH, is derived from the old word,

"Treowth."

A Knight
in shining armor would
"Pledge his Treowth"
to His Lady, and vice versa.
(Such were the Good Olde Fairy Tale Days.) .....But Just What did this mean?

Commitment.
Constancy.
Fidelity.
A Convenant.

Unerring Devotion to Love.
Immaculate Dedication.

In an **IDEAL** fairy tale romance—
(We do not suggest that this actually ever happened)—the Knight served his Lady with deeds of devotion and a Lady responded with chaste fidelity and vice versa. The Knight and the Lady not only spoke of their **Be-trothal,** they acted out their pledge of devotion with constant fidelity and ceaseless faithfulness. Such unerring commitment demonstrated a

Perfect Love,

uniting
the Two as One
in harmonious
relationship.

Please ask:
"Where Oh Where is this sort of
Treowth
found in the Universe today?"

Good Question!

It is found in the
Constancy of the
Sunshine,
The One Light which
nourishes
all Earthly life.

It is found in the gravitational power of
the Sun which embraces the planets of
your solar system in a
Rhythmic dance of orbits and rotation.
It is found in the beating heart
and the inhaling and exhaling of breath.
Treowth is found in the

Endlesssly Repetitive Phenomena
Endlesssly Repetitive Phenomena
Endlesssly Repetitive Phenomena

Such as the Earthly seasons and tides.
It is found in All the Natural World.
The Treowth is
found in the
budding of the
blossoms in
Spring and
in the
Making of the
honey in the
hive.

The Treowth is found in the awesome
**ongoing STEADFASTNESS
of the ANCIENT STONES—
the Oldest Among YOU--**

—upon which you build your homes.

Over And Over And Over, Through Countless Moments of the NOW, Rocks and Stones are FROZEN in their Beingness...

So That You May Walk Upon This Earth!
The Treowth is found in the rotting of a log. It is found in the maggots who in dead Ernest perpetuate the fertility of the soil and the cycle of life in the Constant Ongoing Resurrection Of Beingness in Time.
What more could you ask for?

"I Am the Resurrection and the Life!"

Death and Rebirth are My Dominion.

I AM CONSTANTLY ROMANCING YOU with The Treowth.

I send a Love Letter

From All the Heavens and the Earth...

The Natural Kingdoms are characterized by

Treowth

The Unerring Devotion to
Maintaining All the Lovingly
Co-operative, Harmonious
Relationships
that Endlessly Occur
in the Tremendous,
Infinite Universe.

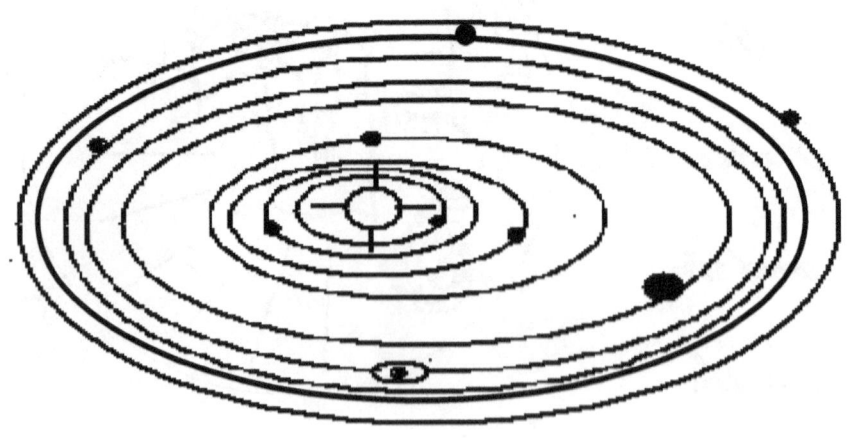

With their deeds of constancy, the Heavenly Bodies and all natural Being speaks—without words—of

MY TREOWTH,
The Pledge that is
THE COVENANT

Between Spirit and the Physical Realm.
All of Nature Speaks of Harmonious Relationship.
BUT Humanity
Defies the Covenant.

Nowadays, materialistic science and its orientation toward and application to the production of marketable goods is firmly etched into modern culture and ideology. As a result, the virtue of earthly stewardship has largely been over-shadowed by a full blown exploitative anti-nature, anti-Christ-like "dominion" over the earth. Corporate missionaries strive tirelessly to "convert" the heathen of the world to an irresponsible consumerism that is the "American Way of Life." Mammon (the Spirit of Greed) grasps at the world.

The Science of Materialism is Mammon's right hand man as it profers a universe empty of God. Yet Divinity is in All Things. If Divinity is not Respected and Appreciated, even in the smallest of things, the cumulative power of Disrespect spells disaster for Humankind.

Alas and Alac,
The materialistic mind of the masses is quite unwilling to attribute human-like qualities—such as fidelity and constancy—to the Sun, the Rain, the Clouds, the Planets, the Plants, the Animals or Stones.

***What kind of damn fool honors
a ball of nuclear fusion?
What kind of God-fearing Christian thinks
the Great Spirit really and Treowthly
dwells and speaks in All of Nature?***
***What kind of hokey New Ager or Indian-wanna-Be watches a
hawk soar across the sky and reads a message there???***

It's okay if poets speak of "babbling brooks."
But few are seriously willing to believe that
the Sun, the Light of the World, is a Living Consciousness and Intelligence
that has made a choice for Fidelity and Constancy.
Why is it so much easier to believe that the Sun is just a ball of
exploding gas haphazardly and accidentally doing everything right to
sustain your life rather than being an actual living Intelligent
Body of Beings, Gifting their Light, Warmth
AND INTELLIGENCE to You?

What makes you so darn certain that the Sun is not a living lens, a channel, a medium or the backside of a black hole from which issues a pure emanation of the Logos from the ultimate Godhead of Divinity? What makes you so sure that the Sun is not the home or body of a number of Divine Beings sometmies called the Elohim, the plural word that is often used in the Bible for the word "God."

Or perhaps the Sun is the Face of Ra (Egyptian) or the feminine, Nunda (Cherokee). What makes you so sure that in choosing these names, the Ancients were not describing real aspects of an Intelligence related to the Sun that has yet to be divined by modern material science?

The Sun DESERVES a Sacred Name for Itself!

For the Sun, the Light,
is giving and giving and giving of its own substance and being.
This is the Nature of Sacrifice—Giving of One's Own Substance.
Note that the word "Sacrifice" can simply mean "to make Sacred."
By Giving of Themselves, the I AM or I AM's of the Sun are Sacred.
So many religious persons in the Christian "mainstream" seem determined to allow only that **I, God, KEEP MY DISTANCE,** after some ancient-of-days Divine Week of Creation—when **I** set the whole kit and caboodle into motion— followed by a brief appearance 2000 years ago concluding with the dictation of the Bible and then EARLY RETIREMENT.

Many give lip-service to my "handiwork" in nature. But the fact is, far too often fear-ridden, threat-spouting Christianity admits to My presence only on Sundays in church, or in the words of a dear but mis-used Book that has been ravaged by not always honorable priests, politicians, translators and interpreters.

I AM ALL THAT IS.

Not a sparrow falls without My Consent.

Lettuce screams but you have no ears to hear.

WHAT'S A GOD TO DO?
WRITE ANOTHER BOOK?

YES, Every New Day!
<u>All of the Natural Creation is a
Book of Divine Revelation.</u>

The Natural Order --the Universe is 𝕿𝖍𝖊 𝖂𝖔𝖗𝖉 Made Manifest.

My Messages are written everywhere.

My Voice rides on the Winds but you are deaf.

Heaven Forbid that you worship false gods.
But **I AM** telling you that to treat every natural thing as a manifestation of a Divine Spiritual Cosmos is to usher in the Golden Age, Heaven on Earth, a return to Paradise.

Come out of your
churches, mosques, temples and synagogues, TV dens, bars,
schools, corporate headquarters, cubicles and factories.
For a spell, turn off your boob tubes and computers,
close your cash registers and ledgers and
know I AM with you
EVERYWHERE,
Unto the End of Time.
Do not fail to Seek Me in the Woods and Fields,
On the Mountaintops, at the Seaside,
in the Rain and Snow.
Celebrate the Sun, the Giver of Life,
the Light of the World.
Learn to hear the Voice of the Sacred Creation in
the last Unspoiled places on the Earth.
Then Take this Example, this Purity back
to your places of worship, play and business.
Speak BACK to Me in My Cosmic Language
with Powerful, Flowerful Dances of
Circles and Spirals!
Many rant and rave at or laugh at the notion of
ANTHROPOMORPHISM, PAGANISM
ANAMISM and PANTHEISM.
These words are used to Label and Condemn.

Yet, these are all similar spiritual stances which ascribe to that quaint (or some might say sinful) belief that Intelligent Divine Beingness worthy of acknowledgment populates the Natural World.

But to be a TRUE Christian, Muslim, Jew or Buddhist, to be a Real Human,
is to also dive deep into
The Great Mystery
that lives in <u>every</u> strand and fiber of NATURE.
The Spiritual Science
of the 21st Century
will enrich all great spiritual streams
with the Awareness of the Divine in Nature--
and of course,
Humanity is a Being of Nature.

Take an example from the "Pagan" Native American spiritual tradition, a truly honorable and beautiful tradition. Stones are referred to as "Stone People" and the plants are "Plant People."

**This is a fine approach to looking at Our Universe.
It requires the constant
HONORING and APPRECIATION of the Creation.**
(Even Disney knew how to put the right words in
the mouth of Pocahontas in "Colors of the Wind."
Yet what do you care for the words of a Disney character?)

Alas, must you hear it a million, zillion times until you realize that you <u>MUST</u> recognize Spirit Divine within the All and then behave accordingly, treating

ALL THAT IS *with the Utmost* RESPECT?
MY LIVING INTELLIGENCE RESIDES IN ALL THINGS.

To acknowledge that My Intelligence is Alive in All Things
is not groveling, ignorant worship of false godhood, idols and evil spirits.
This is
Respect for the Treowth,
Respect for
MY COMMITMENT TO YOU.
This is honoring the Spirit Divine,
the Holy One Spirit of God, The Existor, The I AM in every Being.

WAKE UP!

Remember: The Many, including you, Are The One. You are the Light!

It is your sacred commission, your sacred responsibility, to be caretakers—Stewards of the Earth—you were created to be the

EARTHKEEPERS,

so Shape Up!

Every Tree, every Flower, the Winds and the Rains are due acknowledgment, appreciation and respect, just as is Any and

EVERY PERSON.

Of course, the sad truth is, nowadays, people do not appreciate, honor and respect their very own fellow species members.
What **AM I** doing trying to convince People to honor Non-Humans as People?

What AM I Crazy, or What?

(Better call My therapist.)
(EVEN GOD HAS DOUBTS...but only for a moment.**)**

Hear Me Oh Grand Children!
The "Word" is Incarnate in the Creation.

The Earth is Sacred Ground.

I speak to you with many voices,
in a burning bush, perhaps; or indeed,
in the cooing of a dove or in the flight of an eagle;
in the shape of clouds and
in the appearance of rainbows.
Go out into the wilderness and fast. Take a jug of water if you must. Maybe you'll start hearing Voices then or see My Countenance in the Creation. Just do it. Get outside and learn to love it.
My Revelations, as with the Creation, are unceasing and ongoing. Verily, if you honor the Divine Voice of Intelligence as it manifests in both human and non-human forms, sooner or later you will learn to understand exactly what it is saying—everywhere.

Every rock and stone will start to sing— and you will awaken to your Self.

When enough people do this,
The New Heaven and the New Earth will be manifest in this planetary realm.
It is Your Choice, Your Will, Your Responsibility.
My Choice, My Will, My Responsibility.

We Are One. You are Me, I am You.
AND All Nature bears witness to the Treowth,
to the Covenant of Harmony
that Spirit Divine attempts to maintain.
But <u>Humanity</u> does not play its Divine role!

Look at what Humanity has done.

The Word is Crucified when you pollute, strip mine, slash and burn the rainforests, spill oil and bomb each other.

I Am Crucified Again

whenever a Soldier Falls on a field of Battle.

The Treowth is sullied and defiled,
the Covenant is defied,
when facts are manipulated so as to create a
chaotic, disharmonious relationship
between person and person, and

between people and the natural order of things.
The Treowth is served
when it functions as a consistent
mediating, harmonizing force between
any one part of the "The All That Is"
and another part of the "The All That Is."

In other words, the Treowth is

THE FORCE OF THREE

(The Power of the Treow (Trio))

The Trinity Force

illustrated again by **The Coin Factor!**

*We showed how The Coin Factor illustrates
Individuality--That It Takes Two to Tango.
Without a division of the One Into Two or more,*
There is Little Meaning to Creation. But...
How many sides does a coin have?

Hocus Pocus! A coin has 3 sides!

Heads, Tails, and the EDGE!

We didn't consider this before. We will Now. Poor, neglected, ignored, overlooked

EDGE.

For the sake of instruction, let us allow the Edge to also represent the Center or Middle of the coin.

Now what is the function of the Edge/Center/Middle?

The Edge/Center/Middle is the Buffer Zone, the Neutral Zone, the Mediator, the Intercessor, between Heads and Tails. The Edge/Center/Middle serves to keep Heads and Tails DISTINCTLY APART and serves to maintain their specific individual identities, their individualities. Gosh Durn! Where would Heads and Tails be without the Edge/Center/Middle?

Nowhere!!

The Coin Factor demonstrates that a third element, a presence or power or factor or will or force must be present to mediate or intercede or act as a go-between when two parties form a duality. **The Trinity Force is the "Dynamo"--the WILL-- in a "Dynamic Duo."** **THE TRINITY FORCE is the Great Mysterious, Omnipotent Spirit Divine's Intelligent Gift of**

The Three- 3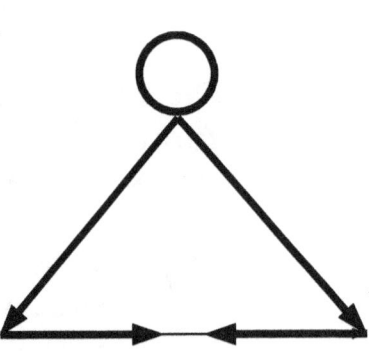

(represented by the Triangle.)
The Trinity Force ensures
HARMONY AND BALANCE.

The Third side of a Triangle--the Trinity Force--**Reunites** the Two that Emerge from the One.

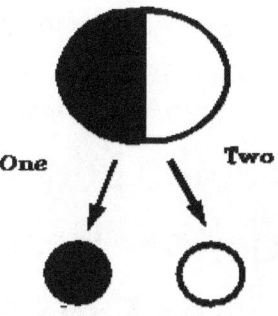

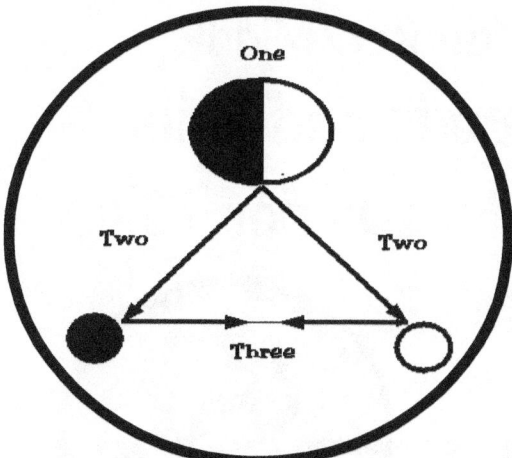

(Of course, at any particular time, any leg of a triangle can be the Third side.)
The Three, the Trinity Force, is itself another characteristic, an Aspect of the All-Engulfing **One.**

No doubt about it... The Three is a Strange

PARADOX.

Ahhh, you may wonder... What is a Paradox?

(Now......We approach The Heart of the Matter.)

A paradox is a statement which contradicts itself and yet rings (and is) true. It often utilizes the "Both/And" and the "Neither/Nor."

In the case of the coin, for instance, the Edge/Center/Middle is part and parcel of the very substance,
the cold metallic "material" for both Heads and Tails.
Yet the Edge/Center/Middle is neither Heads nor Tails, Only.
The Edge/Center/Middle
Is Both Heads and Tails but Neither Heads nor Tails!

ZEN QUESTION: Where does the Edge End and the Heads or Tails Begin?

The Edge/Center/Middle is the place where the identity or individuality of
Heads and Tails merge and seemingly become lost, annihilated,
non-existent or unmanifest.
Yet, paradoxically, the existence of the Edge/Center/Middle ensures and is necessary for the existence of Heads and Tails.
Put that in your pipe and smoke it.

As an illustration for Threeness, the coin is a
"Microcosm of the Macrocosm."
As it is with the little world of the coin, a "Microcosm,"
so it is with the greater universe AT LARGE, the "Macrocosm."

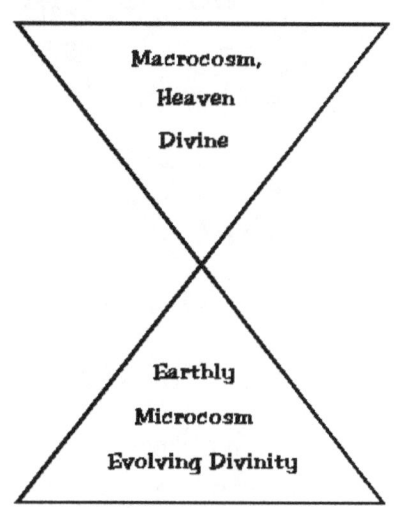

(Or to put it
another way,
"As it is above,
So it is below...
Or so it should be!)

In the case of a simple coin, there is—in a sense
—a third party, actually--

a Force which functions dynamically to simultaneously maintain both duality and unity.

Need I remind you that the coin's substance is Spirit Divine?

In every Microcosm or in the Macrocosm,

SPIRIT DIVIVINE
Holds everything together,
and Keeps everything apart.

In its nature and substance,
Spirit Divine is a paradoxical Trinity Force which is always everything yet **nothing in particular!**

Totally confused?
Good. A little Chaos stirs you out of lethargy.

Let's look at the *Logic of Paradox* a bit more. Consider a strange and rather horrific statement: "Evil is Good."

This is a perfect example of a paradoxical statement.
It can be seen to be both true and false and contradicts itself.

Words

can contradict themselves when trying to support the positions of "The Both/And" and "The Neither/Nor."

Hence, speaking in a **philosophical** manner, it can be said that:
1. "Evil is **Both** Bad **And** Good." —because, of course, by definition, "Evil" is bad stuff, but because it teaches you lessons about yourselves, it has some redeeming qualities so it is not always wholly bad. So, we can say, "Evil is **Both** Bad **And** Good."
2. Therefore, we can also say that "Evil is **Neither** Wholly Bad, **Nor** Wholly Good."
3. Alas, in your Earthly experience, Evil has been an aspect of your experience: hunger, torture, greed, violence. But By God there are rules in the Universe that if you learn them, you can transcend the tragedies that have characterized Earth's history for so long. What I try to show here, however, is that you can overcome this "Evil," through the Middle Way...the Way of Harmony and Balance.

NOW----how about this for an example of a paradox:
Your "religion" should be
<u>Both</u> Pantheistic <u>and</u> Monotheisitic!
How so?   The One Great Spirit
Lives in the All, that is the Holy and Sacred Many.
Therefore, The One Great Spirit Should Be Honored In the Many, in Each Individual.
<u>This is a kind of Panthesim.</u>
But since The All is the One and Only Spirit Divine
<u>this is Monotheism!</u>

EEEEEEEEEEEEEEEEEEK!!!

Something's Burning!
(The flame of Treowth perhaps?)
Check the Back Burner!

The Feminine Aspect of God is Wisdom.

God is the Darkness...and the Light.

Babes are wise?

If everything is God, what about Evil?

The delight of a lifetime awaits those who seek to personify the universal Divine Being of Love that is Themselves and Everything Else.

Overload!

The Limitless Possibilities of Consciousness

247

Remember? I Said:
"GOD IS THE DARKNESS."
Now read this:

Imagine you are seated before a fireplace in an overstuffed armchair in a cherry paneled living room. You are basking in the warmth of a crackling fire, perhaps puffing upon a pipe. Only a rare indulgence but at age 80, you figure, *heavens, why not?* Your father smoked a pipe and the pipe smoke reminds you of him.

Your mind wanders to the word, "philosopher," and you recall fondly that many years ago when you were just a young whippersnapper, your Scout leader bestowed upon you a bit of insight. He told you that the word, "philosopher," is derived from the Greek "philos" which can be translated as "friend" or "lover." And the Greek goddess of wisdom was Sophia. Thus, a philosopher is, plain and simply, a friend or lover of wisdom.

Since that summer many years ago, though buffeted by life's many challenges, you have retained the temperament and attitude of a philosopher, a lover of wisdom. In your retirement you enjoy contemplation, weighing the pros and cons quietly in the bath tub, on the golf course or while gardening. You don't need to read the dense, dry, dusty philosophical books that you found so tedious way back in 1943 in Philosophy 101. You are a natural, practicing philosopher.

Now you are dutifully reading the book your daughter wrote entitled, <u>As Sacred As 1,2,3.</u> You chuckle quietly. *It's about time,* you think, *that someone had a kind word for "paradox." Life was and is filled with paradoxical, contradictory phenomena, statements and events. Things are rarely black and white.*

Take Darkness and Light, you say to yourself. *Why would God say, as He (you're old fashioned and still think of God as "He") is supposedly saying in this book, "I Am the Darkness?" How can Darkness be part of the Whole Divine Order that is Goodness and God, when so often Christians are led to believe that Darkness is Evil?*

You turn to your Bible's subject index and find quotes containing Light and Darkness:

> *God is light, and in him is no darkness at all."* (I John 1:5);

And the light shineth in the darkness, and the darkness comprehended it not. (John 1:5);

...the children of the kingdom shall be cast out into outer darkness: there shall be weeping and gnashing of teeth. (Matthew 8:12);

The people that walked in darkness have seen a great light: they that dwell in the land of the shadow of death, upon them hath the light shined. (Isaiah 9: 2).

That's pretty straightforward, you think. *Biblically speaking, Darkness seems rather bad although it is probably meant mostly in a metaphorical sense. And in any case, you do recognize that Darkness is indeed downright difficult and dangerous. It can cloak the mugger on the street or cause a body to trip on a chair leg in the night and break a hip bone.*
But is Darkness in itself <u>Evil</u>, you wonder, and totally devoid of Divinity? That's really the question. Is Darkness innately,* inherently* and intrinsically* Evil alone and in itself?
   Inasmuch as Darkness can metaphorically represent Ignorance or various other human frailties, yes, it can be associated with Evil. But Heavens, why imagine that Darkness itself is Evil? Darkness is just that and nothing else. Just plain old Darkness. If Darkness is scary it's because bad things can hide there. But couldn't many Good things hide there as well?

You recall that just the other night, after you put the Oldsmobile Cutless into the garage, you went out into the yard and gazed up at the stars. It was deeply calm and peaceful. And wondrous. You wondered if there was any other life out there.

You felt good about the day's golf game. You had played well considering it was 20 below zero. (You are a very dedicated golfer.)

And, now as you relax before the fire, you gaze around the room and realize that the fire would not be so fine and cozy if it weren't for the surrounding darkness of the evening. In your heart, you know

---

*Definititions:
Intrinsic--belonging to the essential nature or constitution of a thing.
Innately--belonging to the essential nature of something.
Inherently--Existing in someone or something as a natural and inseparable quality or right; inborn

that Darkness itself is not evil.

You pick up the nearby favorite volume, *Bartlett's Famous Quotations* to see what sages have said about Darkness. By the light of your small reading lamp and flickering flames you scan these words:

> *A little season of love and laughter,*
> *Of light and life, and pleasure and pain,*
> *And a horror of outer darkness after,*
> *And dust returneth to dust again.*
>   *(Adam Lindsay Gordon, The Swimmer)*

Well, strike one for Darkness there.

You continue reading the words of Henry Vaughn, from *The Night* in *Silex Scintillans*.

> *Dear Night! this world's defeat;*
> *The stop to busy fools; care's check and curb;*
> *The day of spirits; my soul's calm retreat*
> *Which none disturb!*
> *Christ's progress, and His prayer-time;*
> *The hours to which high Heaven doth chime.*

And from the same:
> *There is in God, some say,*
> *A deep but dazzling darkness.*

...And finally, from *The World* in *Silex Scintillans*:

> *I saw Eternity the other night*
> *Like a great ring of pure and endless light.*
> *All calm, as it was bright;...*

You've hit a homerun with *Silex Scintillans* (which you had never heard of before tonight.) The good side of Darkness is dramatized here.

You look back at your many years as a "baby doctor," a pediatrician.

You think of all the thousands of babies that you cared for over a long career. A baby emerges from a dark womb. What could be more innocent and god-like than a baby?

And a daffodil grows up from the dark earth. You believe there is no Evil in either the womb or the earth. On the contrary, you have faith that they are a source of tremendous Good.

As a scientist, you can not simply "buy" the notion that somehow the Devil or original sin has made all Darkness bad. You are not certain that there is a Devil or original sin but those are other questions to ponder. **Right now, you are wondering how a good God could possibly say:** *"I Am the Darkness."*

If there is Evil in Darkness, you think, *it is only because Darkness is just a place where Evil can hide. In itself, Darkness is innocent. Evil exploits the Darkness. Evil uses the Darkness.*

You recall, for a moment, how you used to try to manage the personnel in the pediatric department. More often than not, personnel conflicts resulted from gossip, innuendo, and the spreading of downright lies.

Always there was talk behind another's back and "back biting." Often the offending party was quite "in the dark" about the fact that he or she had been judged, sentenced and condemned. Whenever you became aware of such a situation, you brought accusers and accused together and forced real "light" to be shed upon the situation. You learned to get to the deep, dark bottom of discord by exposing all. You were proud of your accomplishments in this regard, for the harmony that generally prevailed in your department had surpassed that of all others. You were very well loved.

Now a thought pops into your mind. *This book has said that humans create their own world with their thoughts. In other words, fears, anger, hatred and nasty thoughts and ideas are projected in the form of energy waves and patterns into the universe. What if the universe absorbs these energies and in some manner, reflects them back. Then Darkness might be the product of dark souls?*

Your train of thought leads you to snatches of an article you recently read in **The Economist**, which lies nearby on the coffee table. You grab the magazine and find the article about the universe's "cosmic microwave background." It says, among other things, that *"today's models of the universe suggest that it is composed of three sorts of*

stuff: "ordinary" matter, such as protons, neutrons and electrons; "strange dark matter", the nature of which is unknown but can be guessed at; and "dark energy"... "Ordinary matter is only 5% of the total, strange dark matter is 30% and dark energy is 65%."
(The Economist, December 21, 2002—January 3, 2003; The Cosmic Microwave Background, Pole Position, p. 116.)

You close the magazine, you close your eyes and you can almost feel the darkness around you.

Dark energy. Dark matter? What if humankind has created this massive realm of darkness through its own thoughts and actions! You shudder to think. But no, it couldn't be possible....Such darkness certainly predates human history. (Maybe there was a war in heaven...?)

But really--what if-- as this book suggests--that just as the Egoic body is the "mirroring" body, allowing for self-reflection, the entire universe is a mirroring cosmos, manifesting what is projected into it. Now there's a frightening thought! What if Dark energy is the product of humanity's evil thinking? What if Dark energy is truly evil and it is humanity's responsibility? With all the garbage that hangs out in people's heads these days, it's a wonder the sun ever shines!

Uh oh! Mustn't let fear get the best of you!
Sigh. It is obvious to you that Darkness has Both Good attributes AND Bad attributes. It's one of those paradoxical things. And come to think of it, lots of bad things happen in the broad daylight as well!

Well, of course! Some people, some very good people have nice ideas about darkness....they love and appreciate certain aspects of Darkness, the nighttime, the grand and glorious nighttime, for all its gifts. As the poet says,
> *Dear Night! this world's defeat;*
> *The stop to busy fools; care's check and curb;*
> *The day of spirits; my soul's calm retreat*
> *Which none disturb!*
> *Christ's progress, and His prayer-time;*
> *The hours to which high Heaven doth chime.*

You turn your thoughts to some basic science regarding light. Visible light is a vibratory phenomena on the electromagnetic spectrum. But on either side of the visible spectrum is the invisible spectrum. So a space which appears to be empty and dark is likely filled with energies that are of the same kind and nature as light, such as infra-red and ultra-violet "light," microwaves and gamma rays. All are vibrating away but the human eye is totally blind to these.

In other words, **Darkness is often filled with Invisible Light!** Another paradoxical thought!

Well that settles it then, you declare to yourself. *There is no easy answer. The eye limits what we can perceive of the electromagnetic spectrum. The eye limits all our seeing. In a certain respect, Darkness and Light are simply two sides to the same coin of vibratory electromagnetic energy. And if there is Dark Energy and Dark Matter beyond even this...what the heck... As the book is saying, It's all Spirit Divine.*

With the optimists heart, you take a hopeful view. Darkness, at bottom, is a realm of Mystery, Potential and Energy, a kind of holding tank for the Future that is under construction. The architects who design and mold the Future are the God within each human. Like a pinpoint of logic in a dark realm of chaos, like a star twinkling in the night sky, if one so chooses, the Mind's eye can project Light and Hope into Darkness, and be a part of the Salvation of the World.

The Mind's "eye" is truly the Mind's "I ," the "I Am" of the Universe, the Invisible Will that impregnates the Void, the Wisdom that comprehends the Darkness, thereby allowing the Darkness to comprehend the Light.

The Wise One claims the realm of Darkness as its own, you conclude. The Wise one will seize the Night and know it for its challenge and potential.

Suddenly, your sweet musings are shattered by the harsh light of reality. Your wife has flicked on an overhead lamp. She tells you that you had better get to bed because you have an early appointment tomorrow at the dentist.

End of Story

Yes. I AM the Darkness. I AM ultraviolet radiation, gamma rays,

x-rays and as yet undetected invisible cosmic rays.

I Am Dark Matter, Dark Energy, the Weak Force, the Strong Force. I Am Magnetism and Quantum Particles. Some of these you have called dangerous and bad such as the Ultraviolet.
You are brainwashed.

It is your fear and lack of appreciation
which opens you to harm.....For Most of all,
I AM the Ineffable All-Loving, the Light and the Life and AS YET unidentified, undetected, invisible cosmic goodness, awaiting your awakening to your own Power to Create Paradise.
I AM the mysterious forces and phenomena studied in the ivory towers of astrophysicists and nuclear engineers. I Am the stuff of fantasy, dreams, religion, spirituality, science fiction and hard core science.
I Am an Infinite
Field of Potential Behind All That Is.
I AM The Ground of Being, Past, Present and Future,
The Alpha And Omega.
But **I AM** also the simple things.

I AM EVERY BITE
Of The Food You Eat!

I AM the Sacred Bread of Life ground from the Sacred Grain grown from the Sacred Earth,
All which Give of Themselves!
I AM your Home in this Sacred Universe.

𝕮𝖔𝖒𝖒𝖚𝖓𝖊 𝖜𝖎𝖙𝖍 𝕸𝖊 𝖆𝖙 𝕰𝖛𝖊𝖗𝖞 𝕸𝖊𝖆𝖑.

If you do not think of your food as
a Sacred Gift
then you are partaking of the

Impure and Profane.
Your **Thoughts** Create the World You live in.

Take. Eat. The Universal Divine Spirit is My Body which is Broken into the Many for You.

The goal of life is to develop a
Constant Communion
with the Divine harmonics, via the
Images in your Supersensible mind,
the vibrations in your cellular circuits,
the Brain that is in Your Heart.
The Imaginations, Inspirations and Intuitions

of your **Consciousness**...are

Your Mobile, Cellular Connection with the Divine.

So, let's take Consciousness off the back burner.

You all have consciousness, but how often do you Romance Your Consciousnesses? How often do you acknowledge, appreciate, discuss, analyze and wonder about your dear, wonderful Consciousness? How much do you work to develop your consciousness? Do you meditate?

Indeed, for all intents and purposes, you are nothing without your consciousness. Yet, the fact is, most of you take Consciousness for granted. You generally accept it as a fact of life without considering how profound a Gift it is. But what is most dramatically apparent when someone dies? .... They loose Consciousness!

Or so it appears. Actually, Consciousness simply separates from the earthly, mineral body and shifts its focus.

At Death-- Back you Dive Into the Great Sea of Cosmic Consciousness.

Imagine that in an Earthly human life, Your Consciousness is like the peak on the wave of the Ocean of Cosmic Divine Consciousness. Because your focus is on your life affairs, you loose touch with the Divine Ocean of which you are always and forever a remarkable extension.

Sometime after Death, perhaps after lingering with Your Focus still on the earth and family and friends you have left behind, your focus changes and You Realize you are swimming in the Pristine Ocean of Pure Spirit Divine. Other Consciousnesses come to greet you and you commune in a manner that is unlike any ordinary Earthly communion.

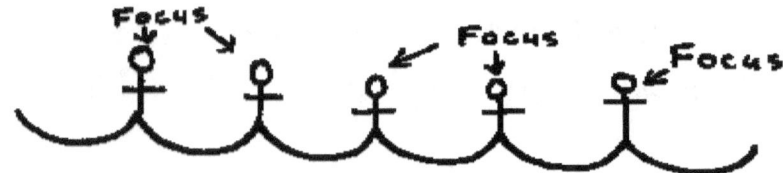

Ocean of the Divine Mind.

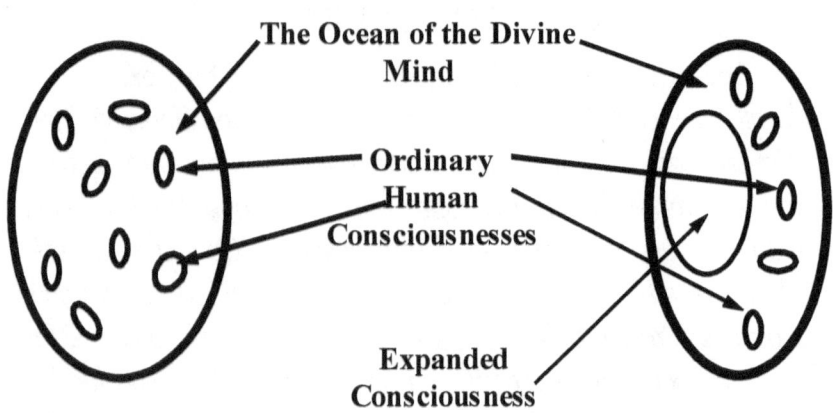

Now is the era of human development when you must begin to think of Consciousness as a vehicle, a body or vessel that contains all the energy of all your thoughts, feelings and impressions.

The body of Consciousness is the receiving station for all "stimuli" that comes to you from the world outside your physical body including all sensations, and the observations and perceptions that may arise due to outside phenomena. Your body of Consciousness (your Egoic body??) is also composed of all forms of awareness of internal stimuli and experience—from the growling of an empty stomach to the loftiest thought you can conjure or invoke.

The vessel of Consciousness contains your every emotion or feeling, every passion, every hate, every hunger, every desire, every joy. The body of Consciousness is the realm of all your vague ideas and careful considerations, all your internal debates and all your daydreams, your imaginations, inspirations, intuitions, your knowledge, wisdom, stored data, programs, memories and insights.

Your infinitely significant Consciousness is the arena in which decisions are made. It is the psychic energy field wherein your WILL POWER resides or hides. It can be and often is the home of the judge and jury and the executioner. It is the paper upon which contracts are made, pledges sealed, covenants agreed upon.

Your Consciousness is the seat of your self-awareness, your self-reflection, your self-identity, your self-government, your anarchy. Your Consciousness is the seat upon which your unique individuality reposes.
It is the royal throne of the "I AM" in You.

Your Consciousness is the Grail Cup from which your

Ego can sip the draught of Everlasting Life.

Your Consciousness is Where You Can Embrace the Vision of the Divine Cosmos.

Divine "I's" Open!

APPRECIATE YOUR CONSCIOUSNESS.
Study techniques and practices for developing "higher consciousness."

The senses of taste, touch, hearing, sight and smell are experienced through physical, material Consciousness. Clearly understand that while you develop your "higher" states of consciousness, I do not advocate that you give up pleasures of the senses or that the bodily senses are somehow EVIL. Not at all. Seeing a sunset is an exquisitely valuable experience. The more, the Better.

Have I not told you to go out to the mountaintops or woods to worship? (Did not the Christ preach in the hills and on the beaches?) I don't want you to go out there, close your eyes and try to shut it all out. No indeed. Bodily delights are a gift, one dish served at the great spiritual feast which can be spread upon the universal table of Consciousness.

But you must realize that bodily sensation is only the tip of an enormous iceberg of Consciousness. Consciousness is an infinitely vast realm. And your personal Consciousness is your vehicle, your ride into heavenly realms, into the Eternal Heart, Mind and Body of Spirit Divine, into MY Consciousness.

Why have Religions always fussed about Meditation and Prayer?

DUH!

You take your Consciousness with you, wherever you go....
Or more precisely,
It takes You and You are It!

REALIZE.

During your earthly lifetime, your personal Consciousness is where you make the willful choices that connect you to or separate you from Spirit Divine. You have the Choice, in the vast region called CONSCIOUSNESS, to live in the Illusion of Separation from the Divine realm. Or alternately, you can seek continually to take part in the on-goingness of Creation. You can partake of Communion.

Please Understand. You are already One of My "Chosen." You are already Eternal Spirit Divine.

But the question is,
"Does your personal Self-Being with its
own Individuality, Will and Name,
does your
EGO, the I AM in you,
make the choice and continually determine
to awaken your Consciousness to this Treowth?

Are You Willing To Make The Commitment to
What it takes to be Divine?
You can work with **ME** or Against **ME**.
But understand.
Working Against **ME**
is a Loosing Cause.
Treowth,
the Messages from the universe,
and <u>Your</u> Consciousness
are intimately linked.
Your consciousness holds
the MIRROR which reflects the Messages,
that the Creation is itself Mirroring.
If your Co-creator's mirror is clear,
clean and not warped or angled oddly,
you'll get an accurate picture of the universe.
But if you are a lousy, careless house-keeper and your mirror is
dirty and damaged, or curved or misshapen—
like the mirrors in an amusement park's "Hall of Mirrors"—
your Consciousness of the universe will be warped.
You may even tune into Dark Intelligences and
Lowly, Ill-Conceived Energies of like Mind.
If you are ignoring your spiritual destiny, and denying that God is
in You, Your ability to "reflect" upon the truth and treowths of
the universe is handicapped.

Warped Minds Warp Even Good Ideas.

What are you broadcasting out to the Cosmos? What is the Cosmos mirroring back to you? Are you working in co-operation with the Divine Giver Who Gives All?

Do you make a Big Deal of the Differences between you and your Enemy?
Do you declare your Way the Only Way?
Maybe You have taken a Grand Idea and Warped It!

Believe it or not, there are people who walk the earth who have
the keen ability to almost perfectly reflect the truths of
"The All That Is," of God.
They are too few and far between. **But they absolutely do exist.**

Would you recognize them?

If you are ever lucky enough to meet someone like this,
you might call this sort of personage
a sage, a wise one, or a Master.
Or perhaps, you might call them "Enlightened."
They might be able to work "miracles" because they understand
how the universe functions.
But do you think they would be so crude as to simply
"show off" with a miracle or two?
Perhaps, if you knew them well enough you would realize that
their wisdom, their knowledge, their intelligence, their
Consciousness of the Treowth is so astounding that they seem
Holy and Divine.
Then again, you might just call them FAKES!!
Some of them might be. But others are real.
The fact is there are those whose consciousness constantly
informs them beyond a shadow of a doubt that
"THE ALL THAT IS"—
the multiplicity of Universal Being—
is itself a sensational, perceptive, perceptible,
Living Field of LOVING CONSCIOUSNESS
characterized by Holy Beauty, Divine Intelligence,
Sacred Wisdom, Infinite Goodness, Generosity and
Undying Treowth.
They know by experience.
Such Holy Ones are united with **Me**,
the Living Unified Field of Divine Consciousness as full-fledged

Citizens of the Spiritual Cosmos.
They totally embody spiritual greatness.
They have so well developed themselves that their personal
identity and the Great Spirit are One and the Same,
in total vibrational harmony with
BOTH THE Ineffable DARKNESS,
The Great Mystery AND The Divine Light.

Am I saying that there are **Christ-like beings** walking the Earth today? In a word, **yes!** You can bet your sweet bippy.

You do not recognize them because You can only recognize what you are willing to Admit can exist as the Very Highest In Your Own Self. Divine I's Open!

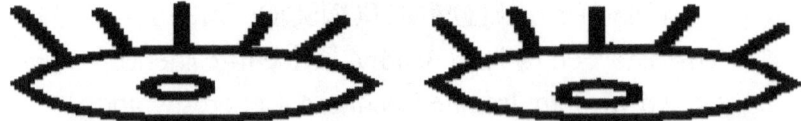

Breathe Deeply of the Divine!

For now I tell you this: The word "Spirit" is derived from the

Latin word which literally means
BREATH.
This can be understood quite literally.
Your Consciousness is the spiritual atmosphere
in which you live.
Your consciousness is the Winds.

My Universe is, in reality, like an ethereal oceanic cloud of Wise, Loving, Spirit Energy Being which Inhales and Exhales Gifts of Trocomth.
I Am the Winds.

What is YOUR Universe?

If you are riding in a submarine, in a vessel of Consciousness in which the air is filled with all manner of lousy, yucky beliefs,
you will never inhale the Ideal, the Best that there is.
You will choke in your own
Illusion, Deception, Denial, Doubt, Disbelief.
If you focus your attention on destructive or imbalanced thoughts, if you distrust the universe's intentions, then you will live in an atmosphere of destruction, imbalance and distrust.
If you permit yourself thoughts of hate, revenge, worry, distrust, paranoia, depression, degeneration, inadequacy and poverty then this is what the winds will bring you. If you dwell solely on material worries, if you focus on belief that disease, failure, victimization, suffering, competition and the struggle for survival are the true, natural order of things, then the atmosphere which you create will be, as it were, dismal, smog laden, self-polluted.
The Winds of Love and Wisdom
will have difficulty penetrating this veil.

This is the Veil of Maya—

Of Illusion and Separation.
This is the Veil that shrouds a tremendous number of human

beings. This is the Veil that they have woven about themselves. Indeed, this is the real clincher: The atmosphere you create in your Consciousness today is the material reality you live in tomorrow.

Simple and obvious examples of creating reality from the mind occur everyday. For instance, an architect dreams about a house. He focuses his mental energies on a design. In a few months or years, if others share his vision, if others reflect upon his thoughts in the mirror of their minds (such as a building contractor) and find them to their liking, the house will be materialized.

The image, the idea within the Consciousness, becomes manifest. Thoughts have determined Reality. This is a crude example of how thoughts can precede, effect, control and, in essence, create reality. In a far more sublime fashion, this is how "The All That Is" functions everywhere. In the hidden, unknown realm, in the Darkness which is full, in the Consciousness of God, there exist Ideals, honorable principles, and Beings who are the Living Representation, the Embodiment of these Ideals.

As I Have said, The Sun is One Such Set of Beings,
One Such Being, the Elohim--many in One.
There are numerous great cosmic Beings who are the co-creative
and (if necessary) the destructive forces of the universe.

They support the Totality which is called the Highest Good, or "God."

Likewise, you little human beings were born with the potential to
be Co-creators with the Divine.
You little human beings already
create much of your own reality,
especially if it is destructive, painful and harmful!
Right down to the stubbed toes
and "accidental" car collisions.
Much of what is conceived by you in the spirit womb of
consciousness, ranging from the sub-conscious state to the clear
state of wakeful intent—is manifested to you sooner or later in
physical reality. But unfortunately, because you pay so little
attention to controlling, developing, transmuting, disciplining,
grooming, beautifying and
Romancing your own Self's Consciousness,
the manifestations that arise for you are often

grim and unsatisfying.
Wishes do come true.

With faith you can move mountains.
But you have to be very careful. Worries "come true" too.
Thinking you don't have enough "comes true."
You are all self-fulfilling prophets.

You and I are the Created, the Creator and the Co-Creator. You and I are the Force of Re-Birth, the "I AM," the Phoenix, The Resurection, The Life.

"Alright already," you say. "God, if you've said it once, so far, you've said it a thousand times. 'This is the "I AM"' and 'That is the "I AM."' The "I AM" is the Universal Existor, etc. etc. But still, I don't know what the "I AM" really is!"

I'll accept that. I expect that.
Infinite patience is very handy.
It ain't an easy idea.
I Am, after all, The Great Mystery,
the Intangible, Ineffable Darkness...the Light of the World,
and everything in Between.
The "I AM" is simply "All that Is."
But I have certain Chief Characteristics...
such as .... the Power to Give of Myself
and to Take Back into Myself.
Indeed, I am Like Fire...giving the force of life,
or consuming and (it would appear) taking life.
I AM a hard-driving force, a potentate,
Infininte Potential, the Eternal Flames,
a Momentum to Be, a Determination to Be,

a Forceful Commitment to Being,
the Intention and Will-to-Be!
I've set My Mind upon Being and Becoming.
I AM The Great Existor,
Consistently, eternally Creating
WHAT WAS, WHAT IS AND WHAT WILL BE.
I AM THE ALPHA AND THE OMEGA.
I Am All the Plans in Heaven and Earth, of Mice and Men and Angels, spewing forth from non-Existence into Existence and Disappearing Again into non-Existence.

Now get this:

Your fiery ego is an intensified focus of this
"I AM," this **WILL TO BE**.
Don't You Feel the Fire of your Being?
If you give the spirit fire of your existence to the

NON-INTELLIGENT
WILL TO BE—
to ignorance—to bad ideas, to war and violence and faulty disfunctional beliefs, you're asking for trouble.

Nasty Side

Nice Side

The "I AM" is a two edged sword.

The "I AM" can be the source of countless "selfish," self-righteous, self-serving or indeed, self-destructive tendencies. Or it can take itself in hand and nourish and love itself and the universe in a wholesome, creative, harmonious, constructive manner.
When you give birth to ill thoughts and emotions, they are bound to take on a life of their own.
Truly, when you conceive of a thought, such as "I hate so-and-so," you have given it birth and given it the spirit-substance of existence.

You give it wings.
It takes to the Winds.
You are made in My Image as a Co-Creator.

When your minds are filled with fear and suspicion toward distrusted or hated objects or beings, these psychic energies give the fire of life to the very objects you fear.
If you harm someone and believe it is okay to do so, then you support a universe in which harming others will live.
Your harm will resonate outward into the future, creating more harm to come. It will come back to haunt you, have no doubt.
As long as you allow yourself the belief that harming is a viable option within the universe you live in, the universe you live in will continue to offer harm as options not just to you but to everyone you meet, or have dealings with.
This will continue until you realize that

"Hey, the Universe would be better if there were no harm. I have learned from experience what it is like to be an object of harm. So I personally won't harm. In fact, I believe Loving is the best solution to humanity's problems and 'turning the other cheek' when at all possible."

This choice is the choice for the highest Good.

This is a choice for Love. Yes indeed, it is a choice to bring the ONENESS God into your universe, to bridge the gap of separation. When you make this decision, you give birth to energies of love and tolerance. When you surround yourself with these energies, you can begin to live in a spiritual atmosphere of

Love and Tolerance.

This can serve as a sort of shield, a "force field," which can protect you from harm, hate and violence. It's quite simple.
I Am not saying that no loving tolerant person can be killed by hateful persons or in a "natural disaster." The course of destiny for humankind has long been established by centuries of destructive energies, thoughts and actions.
There is much "karma" to be accounted for.
BUT I Am saying that the Earth can never become a paradise until it is peopled by Loving or at least Tolerant humans. It's so obvious.
So I AM wondering, who will make the first move—
you or that gay man you judge harshly because he holds such different beliefs than you?

You or your enemy?

Moreover, if you believe that you live in a universe that is random and unfair, where accidents happen, where you can "catch" a disease simply by a quirk of exposure, then by Golly, the universe you live in will remain as such until you see your way clear to understanding that it need not be so.
OR, If you believe that you live in a universe where people are struck by disease because God is punishing them for some sin, then it is not unlikely that you will be struck by a disease for some "sin" that <u>you</u> believe that you have committed.
You can sentence yourself. You can forgive yourself.
God does not punish.
God creates and gives and <u>reflects</u> what is created and given.
What goes around, comes around.
Even Natural disasters are a complex
face of human Co-Creation.

Can the **I AM** that is YOU EnVision
a Universe of total balance, harmony and Love?
Can the **I AM** that is YOU conjure a universe in which light waves
of love are gifting themselves endlessly to the
Creation and to your self?
Paradoxically, you will repeatedly have experiences which reinforce
what you "believe" in—what you imagine to be the Treowth—
until after many lifetimes here or in the universe beyond,
you get it right:
The Highest Good is Love. Give Love; Get Love.
The Highest God is Love.
He Has No One Name but The One.
He Has Many Names.
His Name is the Name You Choose.
The same goes for Her's.

"God is love.
Those that dwell in Love,
dwell in God,
and God in Them."

I John 4: 16

The Divine Spiritual Substance is a Gift for you to mold, shape and sculpt in the Creative workshop of your Consciousness and then Manifest in the NOW. You can create in your lives a domino effect of bad times or good. You can create in your lives a universe of
suffering and punishments around you,
or you can embrace the realm of ideals,
principles and sacred beingness.
You can co-create a universe of love and harmony.

The sky is not nearly the limit.
Miracles are as possible as night and day.
You can live in an earthly body for 1,000 years, or more.
You can live on sunlight. You are an independent, free spirit crystalline ocean in the greater Spirit Ocean Atmosphere of the Will to Be, the Will to Know and the Will to Love.
You are a universe unto yourself.
Pollute the Spirit Ocean Atmosphere of your own Universe, and you will be quarantined, cut off—by your own doing from the greater Universe of Ideals. Pollute the atmosphere
and you will suffocate in your own toxins.

For eons, Beings have been learning the lessons of the Transmutation of Spirit Divine.

The cosmic Creative Beings have learned in their own ways how the universe functions.
They have learned and gained wisdom in their own planetary "schools." They have learned the simple but profound lesson, that wisdom and love create paradise.
They don't buck the system.
They cultivate harmonious relationship.
They champion the cause of the Sacred.
They know that constancy, commitment and devotion to the universal Ideals of steadfast gifting, harmony, balance, beauty and goodness is

THE ONE PATH OF TREOWTH.

These so-called "angels," "archangels," "devas," "seraphims," "cherubim," (and so on) ((and these do exist!))--
and your fellow human Saints, Enlightened Ones, Buddhas and Masters have learned to beget heaven out of themselves.

The high spiritual powers have learned to breath in
Truth, Love and Wisdom and to breath it out again.
They have learned to see that what AnyOne chooses to know as
Treowth—what AnyOne chooses to "believe" in—what AnyOne
chooses to focus the energy of faith and repetition upon—what
Anyone chooses to focus the energy of their mental life upon—
what Anyone chooses to embrace as ideal and pledge oneself
to—what AnyOne chooses to reflect in the mirror of their own
consciousness—will in turn be mirrored back by the Universe
<u>and manifested in the physical world.</u>

JESUS, THE CHRIST, WAS AN EXTRAORDINARY, BEING. HE WAS THE INCARNATION OF THE TOTALITY THAT IS THE GOD OF ONENESS. HIS ROLE ON EARTH WAS

CRITICALLY IMPORTANT. THE DESTINY OF JESU BEN JOSEF, THE CHRIST, WAS SINGULAR AND UNIQUE. SOMEDAY, THE GIFT OF HIS LIFE WILL BE MORE FULLY UNDERSTOOD, AS MORE & MORE HUMANS AWAKEN.

THE ACT OF
JESUS, THE CHRIST,
TO LOVE &
FORGIVE
THOSE WHO WOULD
TAKE HIS LIFE
IN THE MOST
VIOLENT AND
HORRIFIC MANNER,
CREATED
AN ENTIRELY NEW
CONFIGURATION
IN THE MATRIX OF
HUMAN REALITY.
THUS WE WERE

SAVED!
But It Ain't Over Yet
✺✺✺✺✺

AT THE SAME TIME, THE LIVES, EXPERIENCES AND TEACHINGS OF OTHER GREAT SPIRITUAL PERSONAGES ARE ALSO CRITICAL FOR HUMANITY'S DESTINY. THE GIFTS OF SUCH PERSONS DIFFER ONE FROM THE OTHER. THEIR PURPOSES VARY. THESE PEOPLE MAY NOT EVEN CALL THEMSELVES "CHRISTIAN." BUT THEY ARE A BLESSING TO HUMANITY. THEY "REFLECT" THE UNIVERSAL ONENESS OF BEING AND ARE "ENLIGHTENED"...FULLY AWAKE.

And Jesus would have celebrated any who spoke from a heart of love.

AN ENLIGHTENED ONE IS LIKE A MANY FACETED CRYSTAL WHICH ABSORBS THE LIGHT, LOVE AND TRUTH THAT RAYS IN FROM THE UNIVERSE. THEN THEY REFRACT IT AND AMPLIFY IT AND INTERPRET IT FOR THE CONTEXT IN WHICH THEY DWELL. THEN IT IS APPROPRIATELY RETURNED TO THE UNIVERSE, SENT FORTH AND RECYCLED.

From all quarters of the universe, from every direction of space, Spirit Divine shines into the crystalline Being of an Enlightened Soul/Spirit. In this way, an Enlightened One is an absolute accurate copy, a clone, a hologram, a faithful genetic duplication of the Being of God, the Being of the Highest Good.
An Enlightened soul/spirit on Earth is the Virtual Image of God.

It is as if a Godzillion motion picture projectors were focused on One spot and Poof!—there stands the human ideal, an Enlightened Being, a Christed Spirit.
Such a One is an exact microcosm of the macrocosm, literally. (To understand this idea in greater depth, study the hologram.)
For a simple consideration of this,
note that the human body is 70% water.
Water is transparent and at the same time reflects light.
A drop of water is like a tiny crystal, reflecting and refracting the energy called "light."
Every human is a composite fluid of reflecting crystals!
The crystal truth is that you came into the world at birth as an unblemished, pure Soul/Spirit, (restored and revitalized from a previous lifetime on earth) and

as a baby

you were as brilliant as the sun, a moral genius,
a Being composed of infinite love and compassion.
You gave yourself totally.
On earth, you entrusted yourself
to the spiritual atmosphere of your parents.
You joined your Egoic Body with the material DNA Substance of the preceding Seven Generations.
You inherited its genetic flaws and virtues.

(You got a bit of your old etheric and astral bodies also.) Now you may be warped, muddied, scratched, perhaps choking in your own flotsam and jetsam. Nevertheless,
you CAN REVERSE the proceedings or transform them.

YOU JUST NEED TO DO SOME MAJOR HOUSECLEANING.
You need some remedial repairs.
You need to re-learn to
Mediate between yourself and the greater One.

YOUR TRUE AND ESSENTIAL NATURE AND DESTINY IS THE BRILLIANCY OF THE !!!!!!!!!!SUN!!!!!!!!!!

Your True and Essential
Nature and Destiny
Is the Brilliancy of the Light,
The Divinely Created, the Christ.
???????????????????????
You are a Co-Creator with Spirit Divine.
You have a Sacred Message to Deliver.
You are meant to be
An embodiment of the Holy Spirit.
Treowth Incarnate,
the Comforter,

the Intercessor, the Mediator.
Are you getting the Message?
Are you Delivering your Message?

Duh! I still don't get it!
OOPs, with My ability to know all things, I can see
there is someone in Trenton, New Jersey, reading this book that
needs ME to HARP ON. So I will!
Remember, a few pages ago, I said that
"Spirit Divine holds everything together
and everything apart." (Page 245)
So, let's look at just what I do to keep the whole universe
together and apart.
NOW.

WHADAYA THINK I DO?
??????????????
I DO WHATEVER IT TAKES.

So now you wonder what it takes.
The Sad, Paradoxical Truth Is—
Sometimes I Need to Raise Hell
to Re-Create Heaven.
When things get really bad—when there are major imbalances in
the system and the pendulum has swung far enough in one
direction or the other,
The Trinity Force kicks in.
Balance and Harmony are Restored at a Cost.
Yes, I swirl the clouds into the spiraling hurricane and make the
Earth to tremble. I send plagues/You create plagues.

Not a thunderbolt falls without my consent.
When people go crazy—I go Crazy.

My wrathful Face is Revealed, Mirroring Yours!

Did **I Say** earlier that YOU cause the hurricanes,
the fires, the droughts, etc.?
Well, your wish is My Command!

**IN YOUR HEART OF HEARTS,
YOUR WILL IS MY WILL.**

You want to be restored to your original unity with and likeness of
ME.
You don't want to live in a terrible world,
so you are willing to see it cleansed.
Whatever your common everyday, worldly aspirations might be,
your destiny is to achieve Ever- Lasting, Ever-Loving
Self-Conscious, Eternal, Ethereal Citizenship in a Spiritual Cosmos.
Deep inside, under all the layers of warped beliefs and
confused ideas, there is an Ideal Divine human with
a deep and passionate longing

to be a full Firey expression of God!

This Being that wants to be "Christ In You" and
<u>Is</u> the "Christ In You" will not let you rest until it is permitted to
come to expression and maturity.
This Being that is "God in You" will force the issue
EVEN IF YOU HAVE TO DIE TO DO IT—TO GET RID OF YOUR
MESSED UP, TEDIOUS, LOUSY LIVES.
Disease is born. Plagues happen. Death happens.
Even if your life seems okay, but it is selfish and indulgent or
simply mediocre, a deeper INTELLIGENCE WITHIN could sooner or
later kick you in the BUTT and say, "GET ON WITH IT!"

Humans are destined to defeat Death and to achieve an Intelligent Immortality.

You are destined to be endowed with Powers which to most of you today would be called "supernatural." But fortunately, the system operating within this universe--set in motion eons ago-- will not bestow such Power upon you until you learn the responsibilities such Power entails.
Look what you have done with atomic power!
I can't let destructive spirits like you range freely around the universe with supernatural powers! And you wonder why aliens don't come right out and make contact with you?

And your children wonder why there are no unicorns.
You are living this life now on Earth to learn powerful lessons of pain, suffering and death. Through these experiences you learn about forgiving... which in God you would call the capacity for compassion, for grace and mercy.

But No doubt about it.
Not a sparrow falls without reason.
Pain and suffering are the results of imbalances and disharmonic participation in the universal dance.
The Earth is a School and someday you will all be Masters.
I AM DOING WHATEVER IT TAKES
to Create Co-Creators.
It takes a God-awful lot to sculpt an
IDEAL HUMAN out of a lump of clay!

The teachings of incarnation and reincarnation—
that human soul/spirit consciousnesses materialize and dematerialize in and out of the realm of physical form—
goes a long way to explain what's really happening.
Open your Minds to Eternity!
Simplistic notions of a one way ticket
To heaven or hell
serve the cause of alienation and fear,
not the cause of Spirit Divine,
not the cause of the Treowth, the Covenant of Harmonics.

Indeed, **I AM** saddened to think that many of you think that this life is so bad, you wouldn't want to have to do it on Earth again. Yes, **I Feel** for you. Pain and suffering are the growing pangs of a tremendously long process of spiritual maturation. There is no free ticket to the Kingdom, the Power and the Glory.
The gift of Divine Individuality comes with responsibilities
On Earth as it is in Heaven.
Believe it or not, innocent children who suffer are ancient, courageous, lion-hearted divine spirits, incarnations of **ME**.
They are spirits made in

My **Image** who chose to be born.
Spirit Divine can choose a cushy Earthly life.
But it also often chooses an Earthly life that begins
with the odds stacked against it.
I Choose to BE on Earth as Humans in spite of almost certain
starvation, drug-related or genetic handicaps, wretched poverty,
abuse, violence and so forth.
HOPE SPRINGS ETERNAL.
So does the stubbornness of the Divine Will to BE.
Until Humanity promotes Divinity for All,
its own role on the cosmic stage in this sometimes tragic drama
that could easily be called
"FROM HERE TO ETERNITY,"
things will continue to be difficult.
When humanity learns and accepts
the RESPONSIBILITIES OF GOOD HOOD,
THE TRAGEDY WILL BECOME A ROMANCE!
"Divine Wrath" is the "punishment"
YOU CREATE FOR YOURSELVES
when you fail to walk and live in harmony and balance.

Jesus, the Man, chose to die rather than deny His Divinity.

You will not live fully until you Own Up to Yours.

Take the Responsibility!

As Paul said: "...Not I, But Christ in Me..."
The Christ is the Divine Child, Oh Child of God...
the Creation is made of the Flesh of My Flesh.
You are That Also.
Whether you like it or not. Whether you believe it or not.
Whether you are a "sinner" or not.
Whether you can work miracles or not.
Whether you now call yourself by the name of Christian, Buddhist, Hindu, Moslem, Jew, Taoist, Sufi, Druid, Atheist, Agnostic, Pagan, Wiccan, Satanist or Voo Doo Economist....You name it...

Your Destiny is Divinity.

You are not simply a clump of building blocks.
You are Spirit Divine, Sacred—to ignore this,
to be in ignore-ance of this is humanity's folly.
Rip asunder the Veil of Illusion!
REALIZE. You need to become
AN ENLIGHTENED BEING, AS BRILLIANT AS THE SUN.
YOU NEED TO SEEK THIS.
The "Material" world is a sham!
Fie on the warped reflection, the sick logic that says you are
"nothing but atoms." "Atoms" are one tiny face of Spirit Divine.
"Atoms" are Godly Light-like energies concentrated into the
realm of physical form.
Repeat after Me:

"The Material world is Spirit Divine. Everything--The Whole Kit and Caboodle-- IS SACRED, HOLY, SPIRIT DIVINE!"

In your world, Spirit Divine is stretched upon the Cross of Time,
nailed to the fleeting Now you call the Present, which in your
fumbling day to day affairs is severely limited in scope
and imagination.
GET THE BIG PICTURE.

EARTH TODAY IS ETERNITY SACRIFICED

for the Sake of New Creations,
such as Yourselves.

BUT IT IS TIME FOR THE RESURRECTION. IT IS TIME FOR DEATH TO BE OVERCOME.

IT IS TIME TO
REMOVE THE EARTH FROM THE
CROSS OF TIME AND RE-ENTER ETERNITY.
It is always time…never too early.

𝕿𝖍𝖊 𝕶𝖎𝖓𝖌𝖉𝖔𝖒 𝖔𝖋 𝕲𝖔𝖉 𝖎𝖘 𝖆𝖙 𝕳𝖆𝖓𝖉.

Always.
The Bible says: "In the beginning was the Word,
the Word was with God and the Word was God.
And the Word became flesh and dwelt among us."
—John 1:1,14
Greek translations of the Bible offer insight into
what "the WORD" is.
For the philosophical Greeks,
"The Word " is

The Divine Logos.

Early Greek manuscripts of the Bible used "Logos"
which is translated as "Word" in English.

**But "Logos" is the Greek root of the word
"Logical."**

(Of course, all you old Star Trek fans know about "logic.")
Logic is merely the power of your Consciousness to
to create order and organize thoughts--but this mental power is a
small reflection, an echo of the Divine Creative Order,
the Eternal Treowth, the Covenant that secures and maintains
within the Universe the life-giving Harmonies—

THE LOGOS IS THE DIVINE, HARMONIC ORDER.

THE RHYTHMIC ORDER.

To Paraphrase the first verse in the Bible's Book of John....
"In the Beginning was the Word..."
"In the Beginning was the Logos..."
"In the Beginning were the Divine Harmonics..."
"In the Beginning was the Intelligence of Rhythm."
"In the Beginning was the One Song,"
the Uni-Verse of Harmony.
The fact is,
DIVINE WISDOM LIVES IN THE
Vibrational Wave Energies that are both
Heard and Unheard, Visible and Invisible.
Divine Wisdom Lives in complex multi-dimensional, ever moving,
holographic, vibrating Matrices that re-Create the Creation.
The One is torn asunder by the Two
YET Lives On by Virtue of
The Three--the Rhythm, the Song, the Tones...
... the Vibrating, Resonate Frequencies of Light.
Wisdom Lives in Light & Festive Song!
The Logos, the Christ, Dances on.
Can you dig it? Can you reflect upon this?
Most emphatically, the Wisdom of the
"Divine Logos" is not the Logic of the Head.

Divine Harmony is a Vibratory, Rhythmic, Repetitive Phenomena **Totally DEVOTED TO KEEPING THE BEAT!**

"For there reigns the Christ Will in the Earth's Sphere,
In Cosmic Rhythym, Gracing Souls... "

(from The Foundation Stone Meditation by Rudolf Steiner)

Seek therefore
the Light and Logic of the Heart.

True Logic drums out a Message, the "Word" of Virtue and Love, endlessly, repetitively, always in Faith and Knowledge!

Now, listen to the "words" in your head.
Are they defending your Divinity or fleeing from it?
To courageously accept the TRUE LOGIC of One's Own Divinity is to make the Divine Word Human.

The Christ will "Come Again"—
The Word will be
Resurrected in the Flesh—
when Humanity logically and heartily

A Divinity Devoted to the Power of Love.
The Christ will come again when Humanity realizes
what it means to be truly human.
YOU ARE:
A LOGOS INCARNATE, THE WORD MADE FLESH.
YOU ARE SPIRIT-COSMIC INTELLIGENCE IN HUMAN FORM.
YOU ARE HOLY MIND,
Entering Into the Physical through the
ALTAR that is A HUMAN BODY
on a SACRED EARTH.
YOU ARE AS BRILLIANT AS THE SUN.

✡ ✡ ✡ ✡ ✡ ✡ ✡ ✡

Do You Believe It? What is holding you back?
Is there an argument raging in your brain?
Do you hear an internal DIALOGUE happening?
Is Your Divine-Self
Arguing with Your Anti-Divine-Self?
Is your Greatness Being Mocked?
Are there TWO Voices in your head dualing?
Are the Logos-in-you and the Anti-Logos-in you in disharmony?
Indeed, it is in your head where
the "Christ in You" confronts the "Anti-Christ in You."
A battle wages in your brain---wherein
the Sacred and the Profane are locked in struggle.

It is words versus The Word. It goes something like this:

The Anti-Christ, the Deceiver, Speaks: *"Brilliant as the sun? Logos Incarnate?" I don't think so. You are just an ordinary human being. You're not a genius. You're surely not worthy of being called divine. You're no saint. Certainly you are not a God. (After all, you can't work miracles.) And even miracle workers can be of the Devil! This entire book disgusts and outrages me! You should be ashamed!*

This is dangerous territory here. This is Evil. Mustn't, mustn't aspire to Godhood! If humans don't crucify you first for your arrogance and blasphemy—THEN GOD HIMSELF WILL CONDEMN YOU TO HELL FIRE for such deluded, outrageous ambition. Keep your place! You're just a lowly sinner, filthy as rags. You're lucky enough to have a forgiving Father and a chance at heaven. Have some humility!

Keep your place! **Shame on you! You're just a human being, nothing more! Jesus was the ONLY son of God and you're not even close to that.** *Oh, maybe you have a "spark" of God in you...but what's a little ole spark compared to a fire?*

Keep your place! Read your Bible and humble yourself. You need a good thrashing!

The Christ replies: Humans must indeed know their place. They are the children of the Living God, born of the Divine. Their birthright is Divinity in a Sacred Heavenly Cosmos. Each human physical body is an Altar where I, the Christ, can enter in. Each human is made in the image of the Divine Creator. Each human is an eternal Flame, an immortal Divine Spirit with a non-physical Fire-like nature. Each human will ultimately learn to be a Co-Creator in harmony with the on-going Divine Creation.

I too Am wary of false pride, excessive pride or arrogance! Humans are quite prone to these vanities. But I came to create a New Heaven and New Earth populated by a glorious, new heavenly hierarchy, a community of self-conscious, responsible, ethereal beings. This requires nothing less than an awakening of humanity to its ultimate destiny.

Get thee Behind Me Satan! You are the Deceiver, the Control Freak, the Fear Monger who would forever chain humanity to a fate of violence, poverty, sickness and death. Your tactics are clever and diabolical. You have even used My

Churches and My Name to keep the people groveling at the foot of the Cross, the very symbol of tyranny and oppression. You have focused human minds upon their guilt, shame and sin, turning them into cowering dogs. They thereby ignore their awesome potential. Human Being.....Awaken to Your Divinity!

If Humans would Bury the Cross--I would be happy to see it go! It speaks of Man's wicked inhumanity to his fellow man. I suffered and forgave my tormentors to show another Way than that of Violence and Cruelty. I AM the Risen Christ, the Victorious Christ and I long for humanity to join me in the celebration of this Victory of the Divine over the Profane. Human Being....Awaken to Your Divinity!

Cowering humility and shame are distractions from the responsibility of moral and spiritual excellence. Above all, such excellence is the call of the Christ. "I'm only human" has become far too common an excuse for spiritual mediocrity. You are your Brothers' Keepers...that is your Divine Calling, not groveling and praying for mercy. Human Being....Awaken to Your Divinity!

The faith of your Fathers must be seen in both its positive and negative aspects. That faith has served high and noble causes throughout history. This continues. Yet at the same time, religious "authorities" and doctrine have given lip service to love while manipulating humanity through shame and guilt and, most tragically of all, through fear. The power of fear has wreaked havoc with the People's self-concept, their idea of who and what they are meant to be.

Have you ever heard that "if you do not accept Jesus Christ as your Savior, you will go to hell"? This was not My message or purpose. I did not come to spread fear in the hearts of humanity! Rather the question is: "Are you yet the embodiment of Divine Love?"

Are you yet the Embodiment of Divine Love?

Go ahead and blindly refuse to acknowledge that your body is specifically designed to be an Altar for the Spirit that is a self-conscious manifestation of Divine Intelligence and Love. Go ahead and diminish yourself. Go ahead and deny **ME here within YOU** in the name of a cowardly humility, a sad self-deprecating shame or a rigid adherence to doctrine, spiritual or scientifiic.

Go ahead and fall back on legalistic haggling over the Bible's message. But heed my warning. Haggling over Biblical proofs and literal interpretations allows the Letter of the Law to stand in the way of fulfillment of the Spirit of the Law. Doesn't this sound oddly familiar? Was I not accused of violations of the Letter of the Law?

Bottom line: You will never achieve your greatest potential unless you consciously accept that **YOUR IDEAL POTENTIAL IS DIVINITY.**

You want to go to heaven? No one enters the Kingdom of Heaven but through Me, the Divinely Created, the Flesh of God's Flesh which is the plain old real, natural, harmonious, cycling SACRED cosmos, the Holy All-that-Is that tirelessly awaits your awakening. Anyone born onto this Earth, this planet, already has one foot on the road to heaven. There may be a few who will never make it all the way but these are few and far between, in a category of Evil all by themselves. And it is Always, Always, Always a Choice.

Become as little children, innocent and pure, joyous and boundlessly filled with the creative energy of new life, dedicated to service. That's the ticket to Heaven. Dance with Joy under My blue sky! Partake of my Abundance!

The universe--the whole kit and caboodle-- has always been Sacred—As Sacred As the One, the Two, the Three and on upward. The Earth is a world of Holy Ground. But because humanity sank so deeply into material, cut off from Spirit, I came as Jesus, the Christ, to give it a kick start for returning to the ethereal, divine form. My Blood was Holy Light-infused—an energized, potentized substance. Yet every great and minor spiritual leader with a decent message of love and respect--no matter their race, sex or cultural heritage or tradition-- are or were My fellow Servants, <u>spokes-people for the Word, the Christ.</u>

Each human will someday be an ethereal citizen in this Sacred Cosmos— something like an angel. Indeed, each is that now but most are Enchanted, under a spell of Illusion. Humans need to see their way clear to the treowth, the commitment. They need to make a decision to acknowledge their common destiny and common origin. This entails responsible living in harmony with each other AND with Nature. In Heaven, <u>All</u> is Sacred. So must it be in the New Earth.

<u>The Anti-Christ:</u> *This stupid book (besides being repetitive and boring) has things all screwed up. It's contriving and twisting words for its own blasphemous ends.*

The Roman Emperors thought they were divine. And most of them were bad guys. I can just see what would happen if lots of kooks read this book and started thinking they are gods.

And how you play with Christian theology and doctrine as if you are some kind of Authority. Where did you go to Divinity School anyway, "Rubba Dubba U?"

Reincarnation? Ha! I hardly think that's even worth addressing. Of course, its downright blashphemous and wrong. Oh, it is true that people these days go to hypnotherapists and then claim they have "remembered" a past life. Pentacostals talk in weird tongues and maybe that's a vestige of a past life. But Reincarnation is New Age clap trap, pagan, sinful, quakery, sensationalism and slanty eyed stupidity. So what if billions of Hindus and Buddhists down through centuries have believed in reincarnation. So what if Native Americans have also. So what if even the Jews asked Christ if he were Elijah come again! What do those backward, racially inferior heathens know? They don't read the Bible. How could they know the truth? God didn't give it to them.

The one and only way to heaven is ......blah, blah, blah, blah blah, blah blah!!!

The Christ: Your Will is your own. You are free to believe as you wish. I will not overtly override or interfere. Time will tell. Experience will teach.

But do not judge or condemn the heathen or "pagan" or non-believer in My Name. You will learn either the hard way or the easy way that God has spoken through many languages, into the ears of many saints, and MY WORDs are in Good Books throughout the World! I have revealed Myself in Countless Ways.

Indeed, there are scoffers and sinners, the greedy and impure, everywhere, in every tradition, in all religions, in every society. But this gives no excuse for AnyOne's arrogant self-righteousness and sweeping condemnations and judgements.

Do not condemn any One in the name of the Loving God. Look to your own soul. Judge not lest you be judged. Your hate and bile will poison you. Do not preach hellfire and brimstone, for in your own pyres will you burn. Life is hard enough as it is. Spread not fear but Love! In condemning others in My Name, you send the Thirsty scurrying for cover, holding their ears so they do not hear the horror that you preach. Your doctrine plants the seeds of Death, not Life. You fan the fires of guilt and sorrow, violence and wars.

I AM the I AM. Where does **My Spirit** not dwell? I exclude no One, no thing. To serve Love is to Live and Breath Love and no other Will will do.

Indeed, **I AM LOVE.** And those that Dwell in Love, Dwell in Me, and I in Them. Every human One has the choice to refuse to admit LOVE into their lives. But those that DECIDE TO LOVE "THE ALL THAT IS," THOSE THAT CHOOSE TO LOVE THEIR ENEMIES, THEIR NEIGHBORS, THE EARTH MOTHER, HER CREATURES AND, LAST BUT NOT LEAST, THEMSELVES—THOSE that make the Logical Choice to see the Awesome Divinity in All—All THESE are the **embodiment of the Second Coming.**

Of course, the People are not usually able to snap their fingers and become intelligent and loving. But anyone who cultivates conscious virtue is on the way. Respect, caring, tolerance, honesty, responsibility, self-esteem, generosity, positive thinking, simple common sense and especially **APPRECIATION of the Gifts**—these are the first steps on the path to a loving, Divine Christ consciousness.

**Seek and Ye Shall Find. Ask and it shall be Given.
The People must choose themselves
in order to be The Chosen.**

The Anti-Christ: *Oh how you distort scripture! You call me the Deceiver but look at You! What a sly magician you are, a wily coyote! You twist the Word and subvert true Christianity. It is YOU that is the Anti-Christ, not I! YOU are the Evil one!*

The Christ: What is this so-called "true Christianity?" Look at Christianity's history, a record of bloody battles over doctrine, territories and kingdoms; a history of tyranny, genocide and exploitation--a history of Kings versus Popes, Protestants versus Catholics--with thousands of soldiers and innocent common folk dead in the wake of such feuds. Of course there have been countless good hearted souls worthy of the name of Christian. But there have been heinous crimes, murders and persecutions, genocides and wars committed with the tacit agreement or active participation of so-called "Christians" who egotistically claimed they were doing My work! What an absurdity!

It's time for Christians to denounce their claim to superiority and their insistence that theirs is the Only True Way. Christians must ACT out LOVE and UNDERSTANDING, not condemnation. Christians must celebrate the Treowths that are expressed in other traditions. Christianity must be born-again, re-formed and renewed as an Earth-honoring, People-appreciating spiritual path.

All this need not be seen as a diminishing of My Sacrifice or a betrayel of the Christ! Far from it. This is the fulfillment. To celebrate the value and gifts found in other paths in no way invalidates the unique and essential nature of My Incarnation and Passion. The streams of the Spirit fructify each other. Someday, humanity will indeed recognize the valid role that each spiritual system has played in humanity's evolution.

America, indeed, has made a remarkable and wonderful start in creating a place for spiritual tolerance and sharing. This start must be nurtured and encouraged. If you want to call yourself a Christian, wash the feet of a Muslim, a Jew, an Aetheist, a Yogi. Hug a Buddhist. (What's in a label but another human being?) Seek to learn of their path. Perhaps their wisdoms will assist you in becoming a better Christian. Speak to them Lovingly of your common humanity, your common spiritual destiny of Divinity.

The measure of a person's spiritual character can be based solely on the degree to which that person aspires and acts to embody ideal Love and compassionate understanding for "The Whole Kit and Caboodle." The proof of the puddin' is in many Thoughts, Words and Deeds. There are no passwords or slogans, no simple confessions that you need to say to "save" yourself.

The churches and their doctrines can hinder or assist in this cause of awakening humanity to Love and Understanding. BUT THEY DO NOT HOLD THE EXCLUSIVE RIGHTS TO ANYTHING. The true church is a spiritual communtiy of the Loving. The church of the Treowth, of the Covenant, is not a worldly institution with a name. The true Church is bound in heaven.

<u>The Anti-Christ:</u> *Why on earth are you railing on and on about Christianity anyway? You'll only make people* *angry! Practice what you preach! You sound very unloving!*

The Christ: The Christ, by definition, cannot be unloving. I <u>AM</u> LOVE! Ever heard of "tough love?" Is it not a good thing to reflect upon one's own virtues or lack of them? The "I AM" can not thrive in one who does not self-reflect.

Anti-Christ: *Well, what about all the other religions and fanatics who hate in the name of God? What about September 11th? How can you Love those horrible murderers who chop off heads?*

The Christ: Again, many, many others are guilty of terrible, diabolical crimes against man and God. Violence, fear-mongering, greed, hypocrisy, fallacy and decadence are not exclusive to Christians, but Christians use My Name, so here I speak to them. At this moment, I Am calling out to my so-called "Christian" body: Awaken! Stop haggling amongst yourselves as you have done for the last 2000 years. STOP exploiting or condemning the so-called "non-Christian," the other denominations, the other faction, other religious paths because You think you Know Better! Indeed, maybe you DO know better. If so, demonstrate this with your LOVE, tolerance, compassion, courage, respect, kindness, etc. But avoid arrogance with a passion! And Appreciate ALL!

The Anti-Christ: *Yeah, right. Hey Baby. I'm growing bored with your self-righteous Holier-Than-Thou preaching. And anyway, the darned fact is... I just don't believe in any God or Supreme Deity and divine destiny especially like you describe it. I really don't see how you can say that God is "The All That Is," Divine Love and Intelligence and Energy and Light and everything in between. As far as I'm concerned, that description of God is a deadend. Who needs Spirit anyway? Why cloud the well-known scientific facts with religious hocus-pocus? It's all just a big mish-mash of atoms and energies, so give me a break!*

Light and energy exist, of course, but why call these Divine? And how can you possibly deduce that the "Gift" of Life and Being has anything to do with an active God-force that's Intelligent and Loving. Excuse me, but where's the proof of all this Love? Life is a struggle and the survival of the fittest is the law of the earth. Mankind may be evolving, just as you say. But he was made in the image of his ancestry, the monkeys, not some Divine Creator Honcho. Humans made up God when they were primitive cave dwellers and it's time we dispensed with the charade. There is no God. The universe is an accidental, haphazard event, a lucky coincidence! You can't prove otherwise! A human is just a material body with a physical brain. When the brain dies, when the heart stops beating, that's the end of it. Humans invented God due to their own lonely, insecurity in this big wide universe.

The Christ: There you go again. Is that your best shot? Perhaps **I Will** call you the Spirit of Materialism, for this has been your favorite argument for the past 150 years or so.

But I know your tricks. You have many faces. And in this modern era, you have charmed mankind with the myth of Materialism— the program that sees everything as lifeless, amoral bits and pieces and not Divine Spirit. First cousin to this Materialistic program is Atheism, believing there is no God and no future beyond the Grave. Talk about deadend doctrines!

Nevertheless, millions are "sold" on your ideology, your PROGRAM, and it is no wonder. There is no doubt that it is "Logical" to a large degree. Science "proves" so very much. And the brainwashing of the 20th Century has taken its toll on humanity.

Oh Anti-Christ, you are no dumbbell. You are not so unlike me as many would suggest! You, Anti-Christ, are often seen as MY **opposite** whose nature is entirely unlike mine. But of course this is inaccurate. You and I are deeply similar and therein lies your power.   Indeed,

> The Anti-Christ IS Divine Intelligence taken too Far to the Extremes.
> It is The Logos that Serves Only the Self and not the All.
> **You are a clever and intelligent LOGOS, extremely logical.**
> **But, you are a Parody, a Mockery of the Divine Logos.**

The Anti-Christ is the Heartless Logos. You are a hardened intelligence with no firey emotions for your fellow humanity, with no passion for the Other, no compassion. You do not see yourself in the Other. You care only for your self, your own survival, your own comforts, your own power, your control, your safety, your success, your belly, your sex-life. You are a perverted Beast who disguises himself as wise and logical and reasonable. You deceive by using My Name.

The Anti-Christ is Profane Intelligence. You are a mockery of Divine Intelligence because you are all head and no heart. You are a paranoid, fearful Consciousness held captive in the hardened, mineral prison called the skull. The human brain has long been encased in the skull, cut off from subtle, universal spiritual energies. The skull has isolated the individual human spirit for the development of self-consciousness, a necessary stage of evolution.. But selfishness--ideas of self-preservation and self-promotion at all cost-- has run away with your thinking. You are an Alien life form...not truly human!

You, Anti-Christ, are Consciousness denied communion with the supreme harmonic and creative beauty of the beating Heart! The Anti-Christ-dominated brain is devoted to selfish goals and plots to manipulate the human masses to satisfy an unquenchable thirst for earthly dominion. You are ruled by Greed. You have few scruples, no conscience. You will manipulate Facts and the so-called Truth to achieve your ends. You resort to violence. You live in denial of the real Christ, the power of Love and Harmony.

You care not at all for matters of the heart. You seek to hold the human spirit enslaved forever within Materiality--all for your own devices. You hate and fear human freedom. You find contemptible and ridicule sacred festivities of dance and song that celebrate the Divinity of the Whole Kit and Caboodle. You despise natural healing, organic foods and wildlife habitats except to win an occasional political friend or to shoot an animal for "sport." You prefer an exclusive Country Club aristocratic notion of religion, politics, economics, God and Divinity. The better to scare and control the masses with! Science is your slave, your yes-man, your weapon.

> The Christ of the Covenant, the Treowth, is the Christ of Harmony.
> War and violence, fear and greed have no place in the
> Cosmos of the Divine One. In the Cosmos of the Divine One,
> <u>All People are healthy, prosperous and free, NOT a chosen few.</u>

You, Anti-Christ, have focused mankind's intellect upon matter, material gain and technological development. THESE ARE NOT EVIL! The single-minded focus on them IS! The SINGLE-MINDED FOCUS on acquiring material wealth is EVIL. This is called Greed. Fear breeds Greed.

> **For the Love of God...turn your mind to the Natural World!!!**

As long as the masses fear that they will not have an income or that they will not have enough to eat, the Anti-Christ is happy! The Sacred Cosmos is Wealth unlimited. The Sacred Cosmos has more than enough for all! Fear not! The Anti-Christ would have you believe that your car can not run on free energy! Many politicians and industrialists would not want your car to run on free energy. How would they make their money?

The Anti-Christ controls the masses through fear. Fear keeps the masses focused on their day to day scramble and they have no time to call out for freedom. They have no time or energy to demand Change. They have no time or energy or courage to demand that the Politicians make Council and Not War! They have no time or energy, will power or spiritual intelligence to demand a technology that serves both humanity and the environment. They have no time or energy to demand that governments must not rule their lives!

As long as the People continue to argue among themselves about religions, to fight with each other over resources, the Anti-Christ is happy. As long as the People fight each other because of politics, religion, oil, race, gender or sexual preference or because they support different political parties or football teams, the Anti-Christ is supremely happy. The Anti-Christ loves a mass culture of conflict, of endless conflicting dualities. Keep the masses distracted from Spirit and cultivating their Consciousnesses! Keep the masses focused on basic necessities or mind-numbing distractions or war. Then no Power can gather enough strength to stand for the True, the Beautiful and the Good.

Because The People of America and the World have no over-arching vision of a **mutual, loving spiritual destiny**, humanity wobbles on the brink of self-destruction.

You, the Anti-Christ are gleeful. You have the world in the palm of your hand. People are confused and confounded. They have not learned to think with their hearts. The skull of Golgatha yet holds sway.

You are the Master of Intelligence, oh Anti-Christ! You have seduced humanity's intellect. The awesome brain power of this sad planet earth is devoted to inventing the next video game, the next high tech gizmo, the next corporate merger, the next genetic engineering research project or the next side-effect ridden wonder drug, the next best advertising ploy, the next political crisis, the next terrorist attack. And you have convinced the masses that there is no better way of life. They stay indoors and rot. They ignore that when My blood was spilled, My DNA, my spirit, united with the Mother, the Earth. Thus...To defile the Earth is to crucify Me Over and Over again!

If you are so smart as to send someone to the Moon, oh Anti-Christ, why can't you figure out how to have World Peace? Why can't you invent a pollution free car or a free, abundant energy source? Why can you not eliminate toxins and pesticides from air and foods? Why, Anti-Christ? Because you don't want to. You think there is no profit to be had in abundance. You fear to give up the reigns of control. You ridicule and persecute innovators to limit the competition.

To the Anti-Christ that lives in each human--
I say this:

Your emotional lives, your heart forces, are paralyzed, atrophied, petrified, withered and sickened. Likewise, your physical bodies suffer and deteriorate.

Nature speaks and you are deaf.
My Voice, My Word,
echoes through All Nature and you hear nothing.

You are so blind, you do not even see the Darkness for what it is!
Your strenuous, competitive mind games are devoid of spiritual compassion and appreciation for the natural world. Hence you can do healings or move mountains only in the crudest of manners with pharmaceuticals, surgery and dynamite.

The Anti-Christ views the world through glasses of dry, tired reasoning. The Anti-Christ promotes a worried logic no longer in touch with the magical, loving nature of the universe. The Anti-Christ does not wish humanity to go beyond atoms and molecules into realms of love, energy and light, song and dance. The Science of the Anti-Christ says that nothing but suffering and pain, blood, sweat and tears is real. The Science of the Anti-Christ hates "miracles."

The People can not heal themselves with song, with sunlight and color, with flowers and herbs, nutrition and meditation. You won't even let them try. The People cannot tele-communicate, de-materialize themselves or materialize food with a wave of the hand. The People can not tele-transport, shapeshift, withstand extremes of cold or heat, fast for days on end, communicate with nature spirits or extraterrestrials, make it rain, travel to the stars or other dimensions or Times.

The People live apart from Nature's power to renew and teach. Simple Solstice and Equinox celebrations are condemned as "pagan" while celebrity gladiators rake in the big bucks.

The People can not see the spirits of the dead or hear their cries. The People can not remember the many past-lives they have led. The People can not see the rainbow aura around every living thing or hear the river singing. The People can not read the message of a hawk in flight or summon the rains.

The People can not see (nor can scientific instruments yet detect) the sacred cosmic ray that hovers over a woman as she gives birth to the infant vessel that will house the incarnating human spirit. This ray pauses over the birth scene like a patient bolt of lightening, yet humans are blind to it.

The People can not give half their income away and see it return a thousandfold. The People do not know how to Council and create harmony with their enemies.

The People can not live 10,000 happy years.

Congratulations Anti-Christ! The People do not even know that these things are part of their Divine Destiny. They do not know that if they were only to develop their Consciousness, The People could be utterly changed!

The People were birthed eons ago as Spirits in heavenly realms. This was the time of Eden, a spirit paradise. But human Spirits were not content in Eden. They hungered for the Knowledge of Good and Evil. They craved the Knowledge of the Self, the Ego, the omnipotent, ominiscient self-reflective "I AM." They greedily sank their teeth into the apple of Self-consciousness and creativity. They fell into Duality, Time and the Material World. Indeed, human Spirits were exiled from spirit-realms, from the Divine consciousness of The One, so that they could come to know themselves as individual "I Am's."

Oh Anti-Christ! This is your legacy. You offered humanity the Cross of Time, the realm of pain and suffering and humans have explored this with a vengeance. Now, you would enslave them forever in this so-called "Material" World where

Death is the victor. But you shall fail.

Hear Me, Human Spirits!

The Anti-Christ has cut you off from "The All That Is." The whole kit and caboodle has been savagely torn from your souls. You have stood back, separated yourself and said, "I AM NOT THAT." A tree is nothing but a means to build a house or make paper. A river is nothing but a place to dump sewage. You say, "I AM NOT THE TREE." "I AM NOT THE RIVER." "I AM NOT RESPONSIBLE for THE POVERTY of the POOR."....But You are Wrong. If you are to be God, the One-That-Is-The-All, then You are the River, the Tree and the Poor. You are every mother and father who looses a son to war. You are every soldier at war. You are every husband, wife, brother or sister who looses a loved one to Cancer. You are every victim of crime. You are every homeless person on the street and every lonely old man in a nursing home.

Where then are the Intercessors,
the Peacemakers,
the Counselors?
Where are those who will embody the Christ,
the Holy Spirits?

The Time of Your Enlightenment is at Hand.

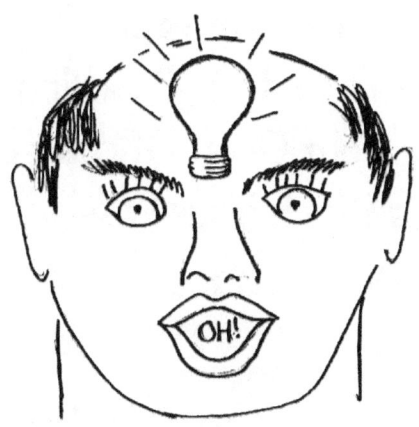

Others are Not Objects. They are You!

The universe is filled with Sacred Beings! Who will speak for them? Who will speak when hundreds of factory workers are laid off so that a cheaper factory can be opened in a Third World country where environmental laws are non-existent? Who will speak for the river where wastewater and toxins are dumped? Who will speak for the cows that are injected with hormones to increase their output when there is already a glut of milk? Who will speak when rich men and politicians send poor men to war? Who will speak for the thousands who sicken because the pharmaceutical companies want you to use their drugs? Who will speak when a Mother can not afford to feed her children?

Are you afraid that these problems can't be solved? Are you too busy to worry your pretty little head about such matters? Do you feel helpless to bring about change? Are you running scared because of credit card debt and mortgage payments?

Then You are a Victim of the Anti-Christ!
You are one of His Captive Minions.
You are His Slave, the Slave of the Beast.
Your Consciousness is Not Your Own!

Oh Anti-Christ!
You have so many in the Palm of Your Hand!
So Many are Fearful!
Do you sit with a Ledger, Counting the Souls you claim for Your Own? Of course you Do!
Quantity is Your Passion!

Fresh water, Flowers, simple Dance and Song, a Breath of fresh air, a kind deed, a loving greeting, a walk in the forest--these are like poison to you. How can these be counted or quanitified?

These concern the Quality of Life.

QUANTIFICATION

is your fatal obsession, <u>your</u> God.
Profane numbers are Your Bread and Butter.
The Anti-Christ focuses on
The Quantities of Life.
Thus, the Sacredness of Life,
The Quality of Life is defiled.

From greedily counting money to callously counting body bags, the Anti-Christ is devoted to measurement and calculation. Thus the Anti-Christ hopes to manipulate all things of this world.

The Anti- Christ, is happiest in a culture that runs smoothly like a finely tooled "high end" computer or stereo. You clamor for artificially controlled, mathematically analyzed atmospheres and budgets. You hover in the wings, waiting for another defense contract. The People and the natural environment groan under the weight of your purchasing power. They bow to your rules that say what food and medicine you can put in your mouth because some company paid enough people to "prove scientifically" that their product was the "one and only" way to heal!

For the sake of profitable numbers, animals are reduced to nothing but market statistics. Cows, pigs and chickens are raised in efficient assembly line farms, never granted their birth right of fresh air, sunshine and the joy of scratching the earth or lolling in her soil. Their lives are just so many scientifically calculated injections of hormones and antibiotics. They are objects, material objects, severed by you from the nurturance of Spirit Divine as it manifests in purity through Nature. They are slaughtered by "employees" who are paid slave wages.

You are dragging everything down with you. It is no wonder that many grow sick on a diet of so many profaned numbers. Too many of your corporate leaders live in denial or complicity. In your obsession with this numerically concise, controlled order, you fear material Scarcity most of all.

So Anti-Christ, you are, in the end, fear incarnate, a hardening force, a rigidifying, paralyzing power. You fear change! The Fall was the entrapment of the hierarchy of Humanity, within the realm of bits and pieces, Spirit condensed into hardened material, into Maya, the illusion. You Anti-Christ, are the opposite of the etherealizing, metamorphosing, eternal, firey **I AM, the magical fire of the Heart...the Lion-hearted--buffalo-hearted Courage.**

Fear is the emotional consequence of the belief in scarcity, doom and gloom. It is the flip side of Knowledge of the Giver Who Gives All, Divine Blessings of Abundance, sharing, community and cooperation. Alas, your fear begets scarcity, shutting down the human soul to receiving from the gifts of Spirit Divine.

Look out upon the universe and see the Abundance. You can not count the stars, the trees, the grains of sand. I AM quite capable of bestowing Abundance.
Let Everyone in the World be a Millionaire!
But to achieve a healthy state of Abundance on earth,
A <u>BALANCING</u> MEASURE OF ENERGY & ACTION MUST BE DEVOTED TO SPIRIT DIVINE...
To Prayers and Meditations of Appreciation,
To Self-Growth and Self-Reflection,
To Giving Gifts and Serving Others,
TO FLOWERS, DANCE AND SONG--
ALAS....

For the sake of the numbers of a greedy productivity, rain forests are leveled, rivers are 'damned', skies are poisoned and vast metropolitan regions are turned to concrete. For the sake of more hamburgers, more dollars, and more heartburn, thousands of pounds of genetically engineered corn fattened cattle are slaughtered without so much as a prayer of thanks.

America, where the Whore of Quantification sleeps soundly every night, has pandered her Material ways to the rest of the World which lapped it up greedily.

Her bounties have become a two edged sword. The rest of the World has eyed America with envy and contempt. All America's other Gifts and Virtues must be rallied to counter the prostitution of Numbers. This is the ultimate test, the ultimate responsibility.

America can embody the ideals of the Church of Philadelphia which is the Church of Brotherly Love, or the Church of Laodicea, as found in the *Book of Revelation of John* in the Bible. As it was said of Laodicea:
I know your works, that you are neither cold nor hot; it is better to be either cold or hot. So then because you are lukewarm, and neither cold nor hot, I will spue you out of my mouth. You say, I am rich and my wealth has increased and I need nothing; and you do not know that you are miserable and a wanderer and poor and blind and naked.

Will spiritual mediocrity be America's most lasting legacy? Or will she embody the highest ideals of Brotherly Love, of Philadelphia? Set your house in order. The hour to decide is upon you.

Greatness of Spirit is the order of the Day!
Balance and Harmony the Key!

Where are the great Mediators, the Go-Betweens who can build bridges between warring camps? Where are the rich MBA's and Wall Street tycoons who can feed the People and end Poverty? Where are the Nobel Prize Laureate Scientists who can devise free, clean abundant energy sources? Where are the organic farms and non-genetically modified seeds that do not require tons of poison pesticides to make money for corporate agri-business?

Where is corporate responsiblity?

Americans can sit back and let their eyes glaze over. For the most part, their material wealth shields them from the ravages of their mediocrity. The promise of pleasantness --the lure of the American Dream-- beguiles them into lethargy. With the rest of the world hating Americans and grasping at the same wealth, where will it lead?

Profane numbers run amuck! Scores, statistics, market orders and TV satellite channels and countless, mind-numbing escapist mechanisms are spread across the globe distracting you from your Destiny! The airwaves are a cacophony of diversions. The earth's electro-magnetic field is as polluted as the water and air.

What is on the increase? The Darkness that is Divine Acts. The Universe Strikes Back: The Divine Chaos that you created must assert itself. Alien Cancer cells, viruses and super bacteria proliferate. Forest fires rage. Summers in Texas grow hotter and drier. Water grows scarcer. Hurricanes rip through the lowlands. The earth buckles and the seas boil.

Meanwhile, the economies totter and the poor grow poorer and masses of the world resent America's wealth and power and eyes its enormous national debt or warring ways like a chained dog that wishes it could tear apart a cruel master. Quality of Life on the planet deteriorates. And everyone copies America!

Debts grow. Terrorists terrorize the world. Fear increases. Bombs drop. Soldiers die. The atmosphere warms, rivers overflow, the ozone dissipates, the Earth trembles. You run the rat race. You spin your stories. You do not hold out the olive branch of peace. You build the machines of War. You do not accept that the outer earthly realm reflects the Inner Life. You deny. You are spoiled by TV shows that you can switch off when you tire of them. Your own Creative Will, the Divine in You, pines away from neglect.

For the materialistic, skeptical, whoring, faithless, fearing Anti-Christ, the lure of the Perfect High Tech Order, the matrix of countless objects, is an obsession. Just so, you Mirror ME, the God who obsesses about making a Natural Paradise of Earth. Statistics and numbers are your manna not the countless joys of the Spirit, the thrilling sharing of ideas, the celebration of Nature and her rhythms, the sharing of her bread and fishes, her prosperity. You see the statistics but not the trees.

You slyly, dishonestly manipulate your numbers to fool Yourself. Your numbers respond to your manipulations and you dally about while awaiting a "conclusive" study that shows you are on a collision course with disaster.

Because for all your accumulated knowledge, you lack true wisdom, the knowledge that the Truth is the Treowth, the commitment to Creating-and Re-Creating what is of the Highest Quality not Quantity. You deny the moral nature of the universe. You do not Believe that Love Destroys Hate. You do not believe that acting for the Good of All is a viable modus operandi.

Your science has no place for Karma, that Good begets Good.

You deny and distrust the stupendous, miraculous beauty of "The All That Is" and refuse to accept the obvious: It CAN ALL work together for THE ALL, not just a Select Few. Good consciousnesses produce Good results!

Material science has distracted, beguiled and tempted all the people, religious or irreligious alike. No one who tried to think for themselves has been immune. The goals of life have been utterly perverted. Science promised material salvation and paradise based on technology and nearly everyone hopped on the band wagon. Thus evolved a deteriorating, collapsing society where numbers, words, the land and everything else are no longer sacred, with the exception of the dollar bill (or euro, or yen, or ruble) and trade agreements.

Marketing wars and preparations for war fuel the world's economies or ravage them. Clean energy sources are suppressed while wars are fought with money paid by the oil-rich.
Capitalists seek labor slaves and drug test guinea pigs in third world countries to ensure dividends.
Alternative healers are marginalized.
"Traditional American quilts" are hand sewn by the Chinese.
Civil rights play second fiddle to profit.
The Earth's environment is treated like dirt.
The meek and innocent, the creatures of the earth, are slaughtered or their environs are poisoned, with little appreciation or few prayers of thanksgiving for their gifts.
Ordinary citizens feel helplessly caught on a treadmill they can not escape, and give no time to consideration to the Divinity of the All, to their Divine Destiny.
They'd rather watch the races, the talks shows, reality shows, the championships, or surf the Internet.

Hey, why not?

Time itself has been perverted.
Humans have lost touch with the cosmic rhythms.
The clock on the wall and the Calendars
are ever more tyrannical dictators!
Time is equated with Money—and
Too Few Spend the Time,
nurturing and loving

The Children.

PROFESSIONAL ATHLETES EARN FAR, FAR MORE THAN
DAY CARE WORKERS, illegal forgeign Nannies, MOTHERS AND
TEACHERS WHOSE WORK IS FAR ,FAR MORE IMPORTANT
than those silly games... endless dualing!!!
The Children do not need more computers or toys!
THEY NEED to see, hear, touch and Love the DIVINE IN YOU!

THE CHILDREN NEED MANY LOVING PEOPLE ALL AROUND THEM...CLOSE TO

THEM!

The children need to run and play in the forests and kick up their heels in the surf. The children need to sleep under the stars and welcome the sun with prayers at dawn. The children need to listen to the stories of the Old Ones. The children need to know how to grow and plant corn and beans and flowers. The children need to breath clean fresh air, working and laughing side by side with friends and family. The children need a world of Peace and Prosperity.
TAKE OUT A PEN AND WRITE IT DOWN. I KNOW WHAT THE CHILDREN NEED! THEY NEED-

_____
_____
_____
_____
_____
_____
_____
_____
_____.

The children need to learn of love and honor.

Now take some time to think about What the Old Ones need,
the People sitting alone in the nursing homes.
Write it down.

_____
_____
_____
_____
_____
_____
_____
_____.

Society desperately grasps at the hope that calculating, posturing politicians can balance the budget and avert a Reckoning and you will all live happily ever after. Society looks the other way when another species becomes extinct, another pension plan falls by the wayside and someone throws a baby into the garbage.

PHEWY!

The Anti-Christ makes a final attempt:

Oh come on! You're really making things out to be worse than they are. Where are your statistics? On whose authority do you base your sweeping condemnations? We must not act hastily. Don't be such a pessimist. Calm down. Things are okay!

The Christ Responds, eyes flashing:
Not One Sparrow falls But with My Consent.
You are Me. Through You only can I work.
In the end, humanity must learn to take responsibility for every last sparrow, every last dead dolphin, every killing, every murder, both human and non-human.

THE EARTH AND HER TEEMING MASSES ARE

SO SACRED!

"The All that Is" must be Saved!
Christ must be reborn!

I AM not about to throw away this beautiful Earth and transport a few rapturous do-gooders to heaven.

The Earth is to be the New Heaven.

Things may very well improve economically and materially. But the imbalances created by exploitation of Peoples and Nature
—And the Denial of Spirit—will take its toll.
Man cannot live by creature comforts alone.
The Spirit of Materialism
must give way to the

Spirit of Spirit!
DON'T LET THE
ANTI-CHRIST FOOL YOU.
YOU ARE
THE KEEPERS OF THE EARTH.

YOUR SACRED DESTINY IS TO CARE FOR THE EARTH
AND ALL HER INHABITANTS.
YOUR SACRED DESTINY IS TO LIFT UP THE MATERIAL REALM,
TO TRANSMUTE IT ALONG WITH YOUR SELVES.
You are here to learn
Responsibility and Commitment.
To imagine that Humanity and the Earth will survive without
the Heart informing the Head
—without an awakening to Christ-like thinking—
without dedicated devotion to tremendous, tender loving
God-like caring and giving—is
AN INSENSITIVE, UNFEELING, HEARTLESS DELUSION—.
THE HEAD WITHOUT THE HEART.

What do you see when you look in the Mirror?
Do You See Your Divine-Self?
or a Skull Covered with Flesh?

☺☠☺☠☺☠☺☠☺☠☺☠☺☠☺

Do You See a Christ or an Anti-Christ?

Are You crucifying the Christ in You?

THE TRUMPET IS SOUNDING.
I AM SUMMONING ALL HEARTS.
HEAR the VOICE CRYING IN THE WILDERNESS!--
Hear the Spring Frog,
the Herald of a new Springtime singing,

YOU ARE THE MISSING LINK!

MATHEMATICALLY STATED:

"0" is the Whole, the All, which is identical to the
"1" that is the One and Only Whole, the Unity,
the Divine "I AM," which is identical to the
"2" which is the Divided Yet Whole One,
the Many, All of You, ALL THAT IS.
The "3" is All of the Many who reunite the dualitites
and Maintain the Wholeness.

3 reconstitutes the One that is Divided.
"3" is the Dynamic Harmony
that Balances Duality.
The Divine Trio is the
Treowth that Nourishes the All,

and thereby Comforts.
"3" is the circular triangle,
come round to itself.
"3" is the Tie that Binds,
the Circle Unbroken.

$$0=1=2=3=2=1=0.$$

The Treowth --
the Prime Trinity
consists of the
Divine Mother Wisdom,
United with the
Divine Father Will
WHO TOGETHER

Give Birth to
The Logos,
The One-Song,
The Uni-Verse.

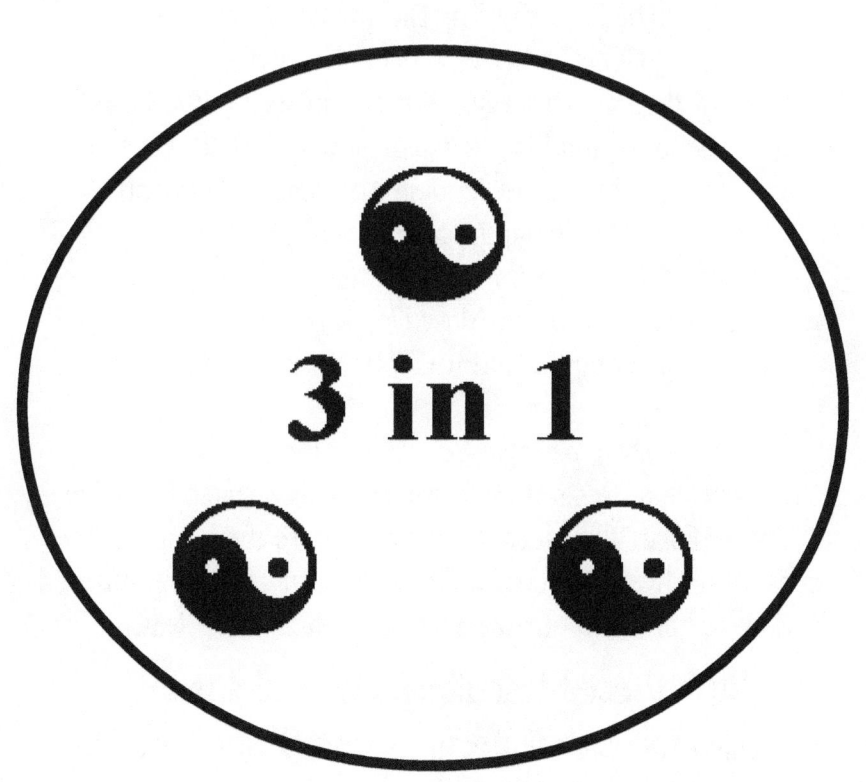

Are you puzzled by The Great Mystery of the Divine Duality of Holy Mother/Father?

The Ancients speak of the
Masculine Patterning and of the Feminine Nurturing.

Thus, the Above, the starry realm, is often associated with
The Father or The Divine Masculine,
("Our Father Who Art in Heaven")
because of the Vast Order and Patterning seen in the Celestial
Vault. The Stars and Planets maintain a pattern of movement
unerringly through Millenniums of Time, in Duration.
Similarly, the acorn holds the
Pattern for the Oak in Potential Form.
Thus The Divine Masculine is Like a Seed,
holding the Potential and the Patterns through Eternity.

In a similar Vein of Thought,
the Earth that Rests "below" the Heavens is called Feminine
("Mother Earth") because it is a place where the Patterns, the
Seeds of All Life are offered a fertile field, constantly reproduced
close at hand and nurtured by Virtue of "Mother Nature."

Both these Masculine and Feminine are
two faces or aspects of the Divine One

that is ultimately Nameless.
But if you like.... you can see
The Father as the Seed of Being,
the Will, the Fire behind the Birth of Anything...

The Feminine is the Earthly garden, the waters,
the soils, Imbued with the Wisdom and Purity
that is seen in every Flower, every Tree.
The Earth is like a Mother
where the Will-to-Be Divine is Planted,
where Human Destiny comes to Fruition,
as Humanity's Time Evolves into Eternity.

And How So?
How is the Seed of the Human Spirit nurtured?
In what dark soils must the Spirit Seeds, the "I Ams," flourish ?

The soil is Wisdom, The Pure Virginal Spirit of Treowth.

Call the Feminine Aspects or Faces of the One Divine God what you will. Invoke The Mother Earth. Gaia. Tara. ELLA!

Invoke Mary, "the Mother of God."
The Ancient Greek Goddess of Wisdom was known as Sophia.
Whatever the name, the Wise and Wonderful
total Commitment to
maintaining the Divine Patterns,
as they metamorphose
from Seed to Flower, to Fruit to Seed,
Over and Over and Over and Over is

the Comforter Who Nurtures the All, by Keeping the Covenant, Balancing and Mediating the Pattern of Dualities.

YES.

Acknowledgement of the Feminine Qualities of Divinity are Absolutely Vital to Human Spirituality.

In the Christian Trinity,
The Holy Spirit, the One who Conceives,
Births and Nurtures

the Divine Child
is the Feminine aspect of the One God,
the Divine Sophia-Maria-Wisdom, the Treowth.
The Feminine Holy Spirit is Untouched by
Human Error, Chaste, Faithful to the Father,
The Potentate, the Firey Will.
The Holy Spirit is Your Divine Mother.
And of course,

You are the Christ-Child,

the Holy One Begotten of the Communion of
Divine Masculine and Divine Feminine,
You are The Existor, the I Am,
Nurtured through Wisdom;
You are the Child sprung from
the Loins of The Potentate's seeding of His Will.
You are The Chosen!

You are The All that Is,
the One who Is Both
THE FATHER,
THE MOTHER,

(yes, even the Holy Spirit of the Treowth)
AND THE CHILD.
You Are Chosen to Be
DIVINELY THREE IN ONE.

Therefore...Pattern yourself after
the Stars in their endless Rhythmic Courses,
like the Heavenly Father
that maintains the Cosmic Covenant.
Be as the Holy Spirit, the Mother, the Matrix of Divine Wisdom
as She nurtures You in your Becoming.
Cultivate the fertile field where you might grow into the
Innocence and Purity of a Child
and become a Free, Responsible, Ethereal, Eternal
Self-Conscious Citizen in a Spiritual Cosmos.

Heed the Clarion Call:
ENLIST TODAY INTO THE
SERVICE of THE ONE SPIRIT DIVINE
THAT GIVES ENDLESSLY OF ITSELF.

JOIN THE TRINITY FORCE.

GIVE WITNESS TO THE UNIVERSE
as it TREOWLY is.

PLEDGE YOUR TREOWTH.
The STAR SEARCH is ON:

Who are the die-hard Romantics
who will Romance the Dualities?
Where are the Shining Grail Knights?
Where are the
Great Matchmakers who can unite the
Dualities, bringing them together,
Betreowthing them in Conjugal Bliss?

WHERE ARE THE MEDIATORS? THE INTERCESSORS?
THE COMFORTERS? THE GO-BETWEENS?
THE ARBITRATORS? THE NEGOTIATORS?

Where are
THE PEACEMAKERS
who, as the Bible says, will be called
"the Children of God?"

ARE YOU HUMAN ENOUGH?

IF NOT...GET A LIFE. LIVE IN EXOTIC PLACES;
LIVE AT THE EDGE OF THE COSMIC COIN.

Who can Exist at the Edge/Center/Middle of the sacred macro-micro cosmic coin where identity becomes murky and individuality is seemingly annihilated?
Who can live Centered Lives,
Paradoxically Choosing to Defend
Sometimes Heads, Sometimes Tails and Sometimes Neither Heads
Nor Tails; and Sometimes Both Heads and Tails,
for the sake of the Covenant?

Who has the Lion-Hearted Courage
to say there are Many Divine Names
when Powerful Voices Say
There can be only One Name?

Who has the Lion-Hearted Courage to stand
Faceless, like a Fool, amidst the Many Faces,
Nameless amongst the Named to Heal the Hatred?
Who will germinate and nurture
a New Heaven and New Earth?
??????????????????????????

BE ALL YOU CAN BE.

BE THE THIRD LEG OF THE ETERNAL TRIANGLE THAT HOLDS
EVERYTHING TOGETHER...AND EVERYTHING APART,
IN DYNAMIC EQUILIBRIUM.

BE A BRIDGE, A BRIDGE OF THE LIGHT,
THE RAINBOW BRIDGE,
BETWEEN THE TERRIBLE DUALITIES
THAT ARE RIPPING THIS WORLD APART.

Who can spread the Word of God while walking the Beauty Way on an Eightfold Path, balancing on the Golden Mean while whirling like a Dervish, chanting Hail Mary, Hare Krishna and Om Mani Pe Me Om while bowing to Mecca, Jerusalem and Rome and holding down a well paying job as a computer GEEK?

Who can parley?

Who can Walk their Talk?

Who can talk without splattering arrogant, self-righteous, intolerant slobber?

Who has the Buffalo Hearted Generosity to Give their Own Lives to the Spiritual Path?

ALL THIS IS YOUR BIRTHRIGHT.

You are a Genius! Brilliant as the Sun!

Be the Wisdom Messenger you were Born to Be, the Voice of the Divine.

BE THE WORD INCARNATE.

BE THE STOUT-HEARTED LOGOS.

YOU DO HAVE A HEART. IT CAN BE
SO MUCH MORE THAN A MUSCLE
THAT PUMPS BLOOD.

Let It Beat Wildly and Passionately for the Virtues that would
build and sustain a Divine Earth, namely respect, tolerance,
wisdom, love, joy, beauty, compassion, kindness, gentleness,
mutual support, sharing, gifting, pleasuring, harmony, prosperity
for all, creativity, honesty, appreciation and
YOU NAME IT.
Let Love Speak in Every word you Utter.

CLAIM YOUR BIRTHRIGHT.

YOU ARE

ROYALTY IN THE CIRCLE OF LIFE.
YOU HAVE LET YOUR DIVINITY
STAGNATE IN YOUR HEADS

with endless chatter and confusion.
Be Not a Parody of, a Mockery of,
an Antithesis of the Divine Self.
Shut down that Chattering,
doubting Anti-Christ!

Embrace The Whole Kit and Caboodle...

The SACRED

1,2,3

of What you ARE!
BE THE

I AM

You Were Born to Be.
LET THE FOUNTAIN OF HUMANITY'S RENEWAL FLOW FROM <u>YOUR</u> HEART.

DON'T JUST SIT THERE
SUCKING ON A PLUM PIT...
sucking up Divine Potential
as if there were no tomorrow.
Eternity stretches out before Us All.
Let's Get On With It!
Do WE want Heaven or Hell on Earth?
Do You want to Graduate from this dang CRAZY
Dancing School of Hard Taps
and FINALLY after millenniums of Earthly turmoil
Earn Your Degree in Dualistic Dynamics?

Let's Make Divinity Happen!

WILL YOURSELF TO BE AN AWAKENED
CO-CREATOR WITH ME, SPIRIT DIVINE.
SEEK AND YE SHALL FIND.

This Uncle God chooses YOU!

JOIN THE TRINITY FORCE:

Positions open for the following:

Harmonizers, rappers, clowns, musicians,
Rhythm keepers, whistlers, dancers,
spiritual physicians,
Healers, psychologists, tricksters, wise fools,
Beauty Path walkers, Questers,
Teachers with Cool.
Jugglers and Balancing Acts not afraid to be Odd,
Relationship Makers, Communicators,
Children of God.
Catholic Buddhist Muslim Jews,
Pathfinders, Community Organizers,
Community Crews.
Intelligent Comics who are not bewildered.
Peacemakers, Poets,
Empowered Magicians,
Diplomats, Counselors, Divine Logicians.
Special Need For Medicine People,
and Honest, Enlightened Politicians!

Also Wanted:
Midwives and Obstetricians
to Help the Divine One Be Born Again in You
—though I Never Died.

Also Recruiting: Mothers & Fathers
who will pledge their Treowth to
Building a World For the Next
Seven Generations of Children.
As Well as MEN AND WOMEN
WHO WILL RESPECT ONE ANOTHER
THEIR ENEMIES, NATURE,
AND THEMSELVES.
Immediate Positions for:
Chauffeurs to Drive the Elegant Vehicles called the Human Body
in which God rides to the Gala Graduation Ceremonies for those
that see a better way than The School of Hard Taps.

Urgently Needed:
Ushers to Host the Arrival of the
Second Coming of the Divine Word
on the Earthly Stage as it AWAKENS
in the Hearts and Minds and
Will of Humanity.

Billions of Openings
for All Who Can Choose Themselves
To BE The

Incarnation of

the

Love

that

will Save the World.

Looking for:
TREOWTH SEEKERS,
Who will Dance With the Same Commitment,
The Same Covenant
Demonstrated When the Earth Circles the Sun.
Who, when they look in the Mirror,
See God and Say:
It is Good.
Looking for: TREOWTH SEEKERS
Who know that the True Seeker Shines
a Light into the Darkness and Comprehends that
The Darkness is also Divine,
for there is nothing that is Not Divine.
The Darkness is the Complement of the Light,
as the Challenge that Must exist and
Always will exist in some Form or Another.
And Love is the PowerTo Make the Best of the Dualities
Of Negative and Positive, Light and Dark, etc. etc.

Looking for TREOWTH SEEKERS
Who see that the time for the
Banishment of Satan, the Anti-Christ.
to Non-Existence has come...
For the Human Spirit is Omnipotent.

Looking for TREOWTH SEEKERS
Who see that the Darkness need not be so Dark!
Because The Darkness is the Limitless Beyond,
an Aspect of the Harmonious Whole,
the Potential of Tomorrow.
The Darkness is the dark womb,
the black rich Earth where Love can grow.

The Darkness is the Inner Brain
that sits Quietly in Stillness and Hears
the Heart of the Universe singing:

> 𝕻𝖘𝖘𝖙....
> 𝕲𝖔𝖉 𝖎𝖘 𝕷𝖔𝖛𝖊,
> 𝕬𝖓𝖉 𝖙𝖍𝖔𝖘𝖊 𝖙𝖍𝖆𝖙
> 𝕯𝖜𝖊𝖑𝖑 𝖎𝖓
> 𝕷𝖔𝖛𝖊,
> 𝕯𝖜𝖊𝖑𝖑 𝖎𝖓 𝕲𝖔𝖉,
> 𝖆𝖓𝖉 𝕲𝖔𝖉 𝖎𝖓
> 𝕿𝖍𝖊𝖒...

No kidding.
YES, YES, YES. SO BE IT. SO BE IT. SO BE IT.
AMEN. AMEN. AMEN.
The Beginning.

Meet Du'Tsu, the Author, (Elizabeth G. M. Richie)

One springtime, some 25 years ago, I settled in to do a Vision Quest on a quiet piece of forested land in the eastern hills of Ohio. I spent four days and three nights there, fasting, and observing, with patient interest, myself and my surroundings. I prayed, conjectured, and slept on the ground.

One night, I'd snuggled into my sleeping bag as the darkness deepened. I heard a rustling near my head, and could not imagine what it was. With a flashlight I discovered a little spring frog busying herself with frog activities. She departed and then a half hour later, she returned and then again departed.

More time passed and the frog made a third appearance! But this time she was on top of an 18" high hay bale that lay right beside me! I was quite taken aback that she had been able to jump or climb that high. Never underestimate a frog!

Sitting in Circle after the Quest, I told of my frog encounter. And my Medicine Elder, Grandmother Pa'Ris'Ha, bestowed upon me the name "Spring Frog." Or in Cherokee, Du'Tsu. (Pronunciations vary.) "She has come to the People to rebirth the purity and light of mankind. Her song is to comfort the Spirit within."

I have several other names, but Du'Tsu has been a beacon for illuminating my purpose for coming to Earth. I use "Dusty" as an easier version of this Medicine name.

I hail from the lush hills of central Pennsylvania. I grew up on a street called The Circle, surrounded by meadows, cornfields, forests. My Huck Finn friends and I loved to play in The Swamp, catching frogs; or we played baseball, or kick-the-can or in the "dirt pile." Or went swimming.

As fate would have it, I was accepted at Princeton University and have a 1975 Bachelor of Arts from the Religion Department. This was the road less traveled. I studied both Eastern and Western traditions and discovered, quite accidentally, Rudolf Steiner's Anthroposophy. So my senior thesis was titled **An Argument for an Anthroposophical View of the Cosmos, Man and Christ.**

After academia, I did a stint as a news reporter and then went off with my Beloved to the foothills of Appalachia. We lived six years in a stone root cellar without electricity or running water on 54 acres of steep forested hillsides. We built a house and raised a family. Love grew and Blessings abounded. And in the mid-1990's, I became obsessed with finding a Medicine teacher, and I did.

In 2008, things changed dramatically and I returned to Pennsylvania to care for my parents. And the story goes on and it's exciting and also well blessed.

Currently, I am a volunteer for The Learning Center for Human Development, a non-profit (htt://lcfhd.org/) founded in 1959 by Grandmother Pa'Ris'Ha, and I'm devoted to our goals and projects. If you'd like to communicate, my email is DustyDancer@frontier.com My website is wellnessandspirituality.net

www.ingramcontent.com/pod-product-compliance
Lightning Source LLC
Chambersburg PA
CBHW021934290426
44108CB00012B/835